NEW DIRECTIONS FOR ADULT A

Susan Imel, *Ohio State University*
EDITOR-IN-CHIEF

The Power and Potential of Collaborative Learning Partnerships

Iris M. Saltiel
Synovus Service Corp.

Angela Sgroi
The College of New Jersey

Ralph G. Brockett
University of Tennessee, Knoxville

EDITORS

Number 79, Fall 1998

JOSSEY-BASS PUBLISHERS
San Francisco

THE POWER AND POTENTIAL OF COLLABORATIVE LEARNING PARTNERSHIPS
Iris M. Saltiel, Angela Sgroi, Ralph G. Brockett (eds.)
New Directions for Adult and Continuing Education, no. 79
Susan Imel, Editor-in-Chief

Copyright © 1998 by Jossey-Bass Inc., Publishers, 350 Sansome Street,
San Francisco, CA, 94104.

Microfilm copies of issues and articles are available in 16mm and 35mm,
as well as microfiche in 105mm, through University Microfilms Inc., 300
North Zeeb Road, Ann Arbor, Michigan 48106–1346.

ISSN 1052–2891   ISBN 0–7879–9815-X

NEW DIRECTIONS FOR ADULT AND CONTINUING EDUCATION is part of The
Jossey-Bass Higher and Adult Education Series and is published quarterly
by Jossey-Bass Inc., Publishers, 350 Sansome Street, San Francisco, California 94104–1342. Periodicals postage paid at San Francisco, California,
and at additional mailing offices. Postmaster: Send address changes to
New Directions for Adult and Continuing Education, Jossey-Bass Inc.,
Publishers, 350 Sansome Street, San Francisco, California 94104–1342.

SUBSCRIPTIONS cost $56.00 for individuals and $99.00 for institutions,
agencies, and libraries.

EDITORIAL CORRESPONDENCE should be sent to the Editor-in-Chief,
Susan Imel, ERIC/ACVE, 1900 Kenny Road, Columbus, Ohio
43210–1090. E-mail: imel.1@osu.edu.

Cover photograph by Wernher Krutein/PHOTOVAULT © 1990.

Jossey-Bass Web address: http://www.josseybass.com

Printed in the United States of America on acid-free recycled paper con-
taining 100 percent recovered waste paper, of which at least 20 percent is
postconsumer waste.

CONTENTS

Editors' Notes

Learning rarely takes place in isolation. Even when learners work by themselves, they usually share what they have learned with others at some time. In recent years, increasing attention has been given in education and human resource development (HRD) to the importance of working collaboratively. Senge's (1990) notion of the "learning organization" is but one example of how this focus can be realized. Its application to the world of adult education and HRD is reflected in a volume by Watkins and Marsick (1993).

The power of collaborative partnerships can be highlighted in a single word: *synergy*. The classic wisdom that "the whole is greater than the sum of its parts" provides the most basic rationale behind this sourcebook. By working collaboratively, learners are in a position to create knowledge and insights distinct from the knowledge each person brings to the learning situation. A collaborative partnership, then, involves much more than simply learning *from* each other; instead, it means learning *with* each other. This is why the potential of collaborative partnerships is virtually unlimited.

The overall purpose of this sourcebook is to offer a collection of writings that look at the power and potential of collaborative learning through the perspectives of individuals who have experienced and studied the phenomenon. In doing so, we will share illustrations of partnerships involving two people, group situations where the effort is grounded in cooperation among members, and collaborative efforts where all members work to create new knowledge distinct from what each member brings to the group. The contributors to this volume approach the notion of collaboration through a range of frameworks; thus, the volume is not grounded in a single theoretical notion of collaboration. However, each author reaffirms his or her belief in the value of collaboration as a means of creating synergy among learners and thus increasing the potential for success in the learning process.

As a guide for authors in considering their topics, we shared a set of questions to be used as a general framework around which to develop each chapter. These questions, which were adapted from Baldwin and Austin's (1995) research on faculty collaboration, were framed around the notion of partners and partnerships; however, authors were encouraged to adapt them as needed. The questions are as follows:

- How do partners find each other and initiate their work?
- What qualities does each partner look for or find in the other? Why is this important? How does it contribute to the dynamic?
- What factors from the particular setting or context affect the success of the partnership?
- How do partnerships change over time?
- What stages do they pass through?

- What role patterns emerge, and what is the relationship of these patterns to the amount and quality of learning?
- What problems emerge?
- What strategies are employed to address these problems?
- How do partners either terminate or agree to continue their work (or relationship)?

In the opening chapter, Iris M. Saltiel sets the stage for the chapters that follow by presenting definitions of several terms related to collaborative partnerships. She makes an important distinction between *collaboration* and *cooperation* and show how, despite the differences in terminology sometimes used, all of the terms are grounded in the importance of the synergistic relationship of learning partners.

The next two chapters look specifically at partnerships in the teaching-learning setting. Iris M. Saltiel draws from a study of support systems used by adult learners in a higher education setting. She describes how learning partnerships are formed, developed, maintained, and terminated. Angela Sgroi, in the third chapter, uses the arts as a backdrop for discussing partnerships between teachers and learners. The role of the teacher in this partnership is given special emphasis.

A somewhat different kind of partnership is the focus of the chapter by Phillip H. Owenby. Drawing from a larger study of the educational and philosophical contributions of the late science fiction writer Robert A. Heinlein, Owenby explores the very special learning partnership Heinlein had with his wife, Virginia. While described as a "silent" partner, Virginia Heinlein is clearly shown to have been an active partner in the broad range of learning efforts necessary for Heinlein to gain familiarity with the many areas of knowledge encompassed by his science fiction novels and short stories.

In the next three chapters, emphasis shifts to collaborative partnerships centering on the process of scholarly research. While scholarly work provides the context for these chapters, the emphasis is more on the process of collaboration than on the content of the specific research projects. Roger Hiemstra and Ralph G. Brockett, in Chapter Five, offer a personal perspective on how their long-standing writing partnership and personal friendship evolved from a faculty member–graduate student mentoring relationship. James E. Witte and Waynne B. James, in the following chapter, describe their experience with a faculty-student cohort of researchers working cooperatively on a large-scale project. They discuss the process of working together as well as some of the difficulties that arose during the effort. Next, M. Carolyn Clark and Denise B. Watson interviewed some of the most prominent female scholars in adult and continuing education in order to gain insight into women's experiences in academic collaborative partnerships. Using direct quotes from the interviews, the authors address several themes, including benefits of collaboration, the process of collaboration, difficulties in collaboration, learning from collaboration, and the evolution of personal friendships out of the collaborative partnership.

The next two chapters bring the volume to a close by putting the illustrative chapters into a larger context. John M. Peters and Joseph L. Armstrong discuss a host of issues and concerns that can emerge when engaging in collaborative learning partnerships. And finally, Angela Sgroi and Iris M. Saltiel offer a closing synthesis of themes and trends from the previous chapters.

It is our hope that this volume illustrates both the power and the potential of collaborative partnerships. Power can be seen in the synergy resulting from successful collaborations. Potential is reflected in the notion that the possibilities that can result from collaborative partnerships are virtually unlimited. We hope that the following chapters will offer insights and encouragement for readers to seek out their own opportunities to learn collaboratively and to dig deeper into this important emerging area of practice in adult and continuing education.

Iris M. Saltiel
Angela Sgroi
Ralph G. Brockett

References

Baldwin, R. G., and Austin, A. R. "Toward a Greater Understanding of Faculty Research Collaboration." *Review of Higher Education,* 1995, *19* (1), 45–70.

Senge, P. *The Fifth Discipline: The Art and Practice of the Learning Organization.* New York: Doubleday, 1990.

Watkins, K. E., and Marsick, V. J. *Sculpting the Learning Organization: Lessons in the Art and Science of Systematic Change.* San Francisco: Jossey-Bass, 1993.

IRIS M. SALTIEL works in a corporate university at Synovus Service Corp., Columbus, Georgia.

ANGELA SGROI is executive assistant to the vice president for academic affairs at The College of New Jersey, working primarily to support faculty research and teaching.

RALPH G. BROCKETT is professor of adult education at the University of Tennessee, Knoxville, and former editor-in-chief of New Directions for Adult and Continuing Education.

This chapter offers a foundation for understanding the nature, scope,
and meaning of collaborative partnerships.

Defining Collaborative Partnerships

Iris M. Saltiel

There is magic in a collaborative partnership. It provides the power to transform ordinary learning experiences into dynamic relationships, resulting in a synergistic process of accomplishment. Descriptions of this type of relationship and its characteristics have defied concise portrayal. We know it when we see it. We can tell when we see a successful partnership in practice. We instinctively know that collaborative partners in learning help each other to achieve what they never could have done on their own.

This chapter sets the stage for the concepts presented in this sourcebook and briefly reviews works whose ideas provide insight into collaborative partnerships in adult learning. Throughout this volume, these concepts will be illuminated in different learning contexts with individuals who are pursuing a variety of goals and objectives.

There are a great many references in the literature to various learning relationships that address aspects of collaborative learning. However, there is not a consensus regarding definitions of different concepts or terms. This contributes to a certain measure of confusion in discussions and sometimes creates the illusion of equivalence or difference when things are not quite that way. Thus in discussions, the framework of collaborative learning ideas is presented through varied interpretations of the terms and definitions.

Almost all the literature on how partnered relationships support adult learning pertains to institutionalized or formally structured relationships, including mentorships, collaborations, and teams, some of which are described in this sourcebook. The nature of this literature also tends to be descriptive. As a result, although they do not focus directly on the interactions between the individuals or on how the partnerships are formed, these works do offer insight into the nature of the personal relationships that so strongly drive motivation and learning.

This chapter briefly reviews the work of writers and thinkers whose ideas provide insights that help us define collaborative learning partnerships. It is my hope that readers will each understand and synthesize this sourcebook's shared views on collaborative learning processes in adult learning in their own way. Our definitions begin with what is meant when we say, "collaborative learning partnerships."

Collaborative Learning Partnerships

The distinguishing feature of collaborative learning partnerships is that the relationship is as important as the knowledge being sought. It is the interaction of the collaborators who work together that becomes valued and potentiates the learning. As the concept is used in this work, collaborative partnerships have at their core an intense relationship centered on mutual goals. It is the social and psychological aspects of working together that are critical in understanding the concepts associated with partnered learning. It is not just that the knowledge is arrived at by people working together, but that the value of that wisdom is construed within the social reality of the partnership as well as the greater social context in which the partnership exists. The essence of partnered learning is that the goal may not have been achieved without the relationship. This perception is validated by the comments of people who have been in a collaborative learning partnership. Wildavsky (1986) helps us to distinguish the fine line between collaborators and partners, specifying that individuals in a collaboration often will have mixed motives and goals whereas partners in learning hold the same goal.

Wildavsky (1986) distinguishes between cooperation and collaboration in his work on collaboration in academic research. He defines cooperation as necessary to get the job done, but different from collaboration because the purpose of collaboration is for "the participants to make use of each other's talents to do what they either could not have done at all or as well alone," (p. 237). This is the essence of collaborative partnership.

Wildavsky's work is based on the relationships between researchers who conduct research together. He speaks of research as a collaboration because it involves working with and through others in the pursuit of new knowledge. From his examination of the process of researchers collaborating, the defining characteristic of collaborative relationships emerges: "Generosity defined as the ability to impose on each other, to do more than half of the work, to rescue each other from one another," (1986, p. 239).This example also illustrates how partners work together. Wildavsky describes other characteristics of collaborative partners, such as the ability to both give and follow directions and the capacity to visualize the progression of activity. He aptly defines the capacity to visualize the progression of activity as the "conjunction of idea and opportunity" (Wildavsky, 1986, p. 241). His description of two people who do better together than alone is at the heart of collaborative partnerships. He also focuses on the dynamic interchange that further defines the roles and relationship of the collaborators. In practical terms, he describes how one writer will reduce the size of a draft, while the other increases it.

Baldwin and Austin (1995) address collaboration among faculty members in their work. They seek to develop a grounded theory of collaboration and to explore how faculty members collaborate as researchers in the academy. By focusing on how researchers as collaborators initiate and experience their relationships, they also contribute to our understanding of the key characteristics of partners who work together. "Collaboration works best when partners/team members share a common mission, have clear goals, define operating guidelines, provide mutual support, and work in an atmosphere of trust, respect, and affection (Baldwin and Austin, 1995, p. 55). Their research points out how each collaborative partnership is unique. Based on their research, they delineate the dynamics used by faculty collaborators to define their relationship and the process of working together. These dynamics provide a foundation as well as a comparison of ideas for us to move forward from.

Collaboration. Collaboration is people working side by side on a joint endeavor. On an organizational level, it is viewed as a strategy for accomplishing systematic change (Kerka, 1997). The key to successful collaboration, according to Kerka (1997), is that the people involved be personally committed to working collaboratively, within a relationship that includes patience, trust, and the awareness that the goals will take time to accomplish. These goals are the same for individuals working in collaborations that occur without organizational support.

In describing faculty collaboration, Baldwin and Austin (1995) rely on the theory of negotiated order to explain how the definition of faculty work evolves over a period of time. Negotiated order "refers to a social context in which relationships are negotiated and renegotiated" (Baldwin and Austin, 1995, p. 59). This theory explains the collaborative process as allowing the individuals involved in collaboration to negotiate their roles, processes of decision making, goals, and methods of communication over time.

Collaborative Learning. Sooner or later any discussion of collaboration in education has to address collaborative learning. Just what is the difference between collaboration and collaborative learning? Is one a subset of the other? From our perspective in this sourcebook, collaboration is organizational or individual entities coming together to work toward a common goal or vision. In collaborative learning, the goal is the acquisition or construction of new knowledge. Peters and Armstrong, in Chapter Eight of this sourcebook, explore more fully this concept of collaborative learning as people working together to construct knowledge. However, collaborative learning is most commonly discussed as a means of fostering active learning in small-group settings. Kenneth Brufee (1993) examines learning among college-level students in a setting where faculty divided students into small groups assigned a group task. Brufee identifies the concept of "craft of interdependence," describing how collaborative learning provides students with an opportunity to work together and to "learn to construct knowledge as it is constructed in the academic disciplines and professions."

Many educators have found collaborative learning to be more successful in promoting achievement than either individualized or competitive learning experiences (Gerlach, 1994). Certainly there is much anecdotal belief that collaboration among learners strengthens the learning. Central to this sourcebook is the conviction that collaboration among learners occurs when the goal is learning, but more so when achieving a goal is deemed unachievable without another person equally committed.

Partnerships

Much of the intellectual and personal growth of the adult learner develops out of personal relationships. These learning relationships take many different forms. Some are with peers, some with mentors, teachers, colleagues, or even mates. Our search for commonalities among these different types of learning relationships revealed typical characteristics of partners in learning. These characteristics help define the concept of *partners in learning* that is central to this sourcebook. In an earlier work, we identified the key traits of personal relationships that became learning partnerships (Saltiel and Sgroi, 1996). The basis of these elements is that partners help each other to see and do what they would never have been able to see or do on their own. The elements of a relationship between partners in learning are as follows (Saltiel and Sgroi, 1996):

Shared goal or purpose
Trust, respect, and loyalty
Personality traits and qualities that are complementary
Respect for each other
Synergy between the partners
A valued relationship

These elements help us appreciate the differentiation and complexity that exists among the types of relationships in pursuit of knowledge. Partners in learning exemplify collaborative learning. Collaborators who are partners support each other and are not just invested in the outcome of the learning venture. Knowledge, power, and assistance are shared reciprocally. The role may be predefined by the partners, or it may evolve in a serendipitous manner. The relationship is alive and vibrant. The relationship is significant because of the value the learner places on the partner. The relationship empowers the partners in learning to achieve more than they set out to do as individuals. This is what is known as synergy. The partners fuel one another, creating an energized dynamic, electric in its feel.

Partners in learning are different from mentoring relationships or teams, which are also considered collaborative partnerships. A defining contrast: partners are equals who select one another with the expectation that they will learn from one another; the basic premise in a mentor-protégé relationship is that the two are not equal and that the protégé will learn from the mentor. The primary difference between teams and partners is that partners self-select and hold a very deep commitment to one another as well as to the success of the endeavor. Individuals can be assigned to a team and have a commitment to the success of the endeavor with no requirement of commitment to others on the team. To better appreciate these different types of learning relationships, let's take a look at where these terms originated.

Mentoring. Much of the literature on learning partners begins with the mentor-protégé relationship. The importance of the mentor's function is revealed in the relationship that defined the role. In Homer's *Odyssey*, Mentor, an old friend of Odysseus, counsels Odysseus's son Telemachus during Odysseus's ten-year absence from home. What could be more intimate than one man's assuming the role of nurturing instructor to the child of his long-missing friend? This archetypal relationship has been emulated or longed for by learners ever since. The role of mentor assumed considerable prominence in the writings of adult educators during the 1980s. During that time, it was the focus of much attention from researchers who began to outline the highly significant and personal contributions these relationships made to learning (Merriam, 1983). This attention led to efforts by many to institutionalize and formalize the mentoring relationship. The significance of the personal relationship between student and mentor has been stressed throughout history and in the literature (see, for example, Cohen, 1995; Daloz, 1986; Galbraith and Cohen; 1995; Levinson, 1978; Merriam, 1983).

The evolution from mentor to learning partner is a natural transition for individuals in a specific relationship and also for the structure of learning relationships. What starts as a learning partnership of two who are not equals (for example, graduate student and faculty adviser) can evolve into a collaborative partnership. In time, the junior member of the partnership grows in stature and experience and becomes a peer of the original mentor, as is illustrated by Hiemstra and Brockett in Chapter Five. Similarly, Baldwin and Austin (1995) studied eighteen university faculty members involved in successful collaborative research and found that seven of these began as professor–graduate student relationships. All were relationships in which the individual members determined the boundaries of their relationship. The various teams differed in terms of roles and responsibilities, standards and expectations, and whether the relationship was both personal and professional. With maturation of the junior member, the relationships changed to reflect a partnership in which the members saw each other more as equals.

Mentor relationships can develop into partnerships. Yet it is important to recognize that the individuals are not on equal footing because mentoring implies that there is a junior member or protégé who admires and learns from the senior member (DeCoster and Brown, 1982). Once the relationship changes to one based on mutual respect, admiration, and encouragement, the relationship progresses to that of partners in learning.

Team Learning. Closer yet to our definition of partners in learning is the concept of team learning. A team, according to Katzenbach and Smith (1993,

p. 45) is "a small number of people with complementary skills who are committed to a common purpose, performance goals, and approach for which they hold themselves mutually accountable." Notable distinctions between partners in learning and teams include the following: partners select each other, while a team can be organized by an outside individual; partners trust one another implicitly and are loyal to each other, while team members may have loyalty to the project and not each other; in partnerships the synergistic quality inherent in the relationship creates a relationship that is deeply valued as part of the endeavor, while in teams the focal point is the work product. These differences, however, do not prevent team members from having personal loyalties to each other. In keeping with Wildavsky's view of collaboration, team learning focuses on the complementary talents of the participants.

Other works on partnered learning (McNeil, 1994; Imel, 1994) present a different definition, defining partners in learning as students who are paired by their teachers. Adding to the confusion is McNeil (1994), who also uses "partners in learning" to mean students who are trained to be peer tutors and work with other students. These other definitions highlight the differences in current terminology.

Conclusion

This volume is concerned with individuals in special relationships that inspire collaborative partnership in learning. Key to our definition of collaborative partners in learning is that these partners select each other. The contributors explore types of partnerships that people create to bring about this synergistic magic. Each chapter provides a perspective on the attributes of partners that are found when people work together toward a common goal. Thus, this mysterious key element that is known yet unknown is the human factor portrayed in this sourcebook; we call it the power of collaborative partnerships in adult learning. The reader will find authors illustrating the concept with wonderful examples of the power of collaborative partnerships in adult learning.

References

Baldwin, R. G., and Austin, A. R. "Toward a Greater Understanding of Faculty Research Collaboration." *Review of Higher Education,* 1995, *19* (1), 45–70.

Brufee, K. A. *Collaborative Learning, Higher Education, Interdependence and the Authority of Knowledge.* Baltimore: Johns Hopkins University Press, 1993.

Cohen, N. H. *Mentoring Adult Learners: A Guide for Educators and Trainers.* Malabar, Fla.: Krieger, 1995.

Daloz, L. A. *Effective Teaching and Mentoring: Realizing the Transformational Power of Adult Learning Experiences.* San Francisco: Jossey-Bass, 1986.

DeCoster, D. A., and Brown, R. D. "Mentoring Relationships and the Educational Process." In R. D. Brown and D. A. DeCoster (eds.), *Mentoring-Transcript Systems for Promoting Student Growth.* New Directions for Student Services, no. 19. San Francisco: Jossey-Bass, 1982.

Galbraith, M. W., and Cohen, N. H. (eds.). *Mentoring: New Strategies and Challenges.* New Directions for Adult and Continuing Education, no. 66. San Francisco: Jossey-Bass, 1995.

Gerlach, J. M. "Is This Collaboration?" In K. Bosworth and S. J. Hamilton (eds.), *Collaborative Learning and Teaching*. New Directions for Teaching and Learning, no. 59. San Francisco: Jossey-Bass, 1994.

Imel, S. *Peer Tutoring in Adult Basic and Literacy Education*. ERIC Digest No. 146. Columbus: ERIC Clearinghouse on Adult, Career, and Vocational Education, Center on Education and Training for Employment, The Ohio State University, 1994.

Katzenbach, J. R., and Smith, D. K. *The Wisdom of Teams: Creating the High-Performance Organization*. Boston: Harvard Business School Press, 1993.

Kerka, S. *Developing Collaborative Partnerships*. Columbus: ERIC Clearinghouse on Adult, Career, and Vocational Education, Center on Education and Training for Employment, Ohio State University, 1997.

Levinson, D. J. *The Seasons of a Man's Life*. New York: Knopf, 1978.

McNeil, M. "Creating Powerful Partnerships Through Partner Learning," In J. S. Thousand, R. A. Villa, and A. I. Nevin (eds.), *Creativity and Collaborative Learning: A Practical Guide to Empowering Students and Teachers*. Baltimore: Brookes, 1994.

Merriam, S. B. "Mentors and Protégés: A Critical Review of the Literature." *Adult Education Quarterly*, 1983, 33 (3), 161–173.

Saltiel, I. M., and Sgroi, A. "The Power of the Partner in Adult Learning." Presentation at the American Association for Adult and Continuing Education conference, Charlotte, N.C., Nov. 1996.

Wildavsky, A. "On Collaboration." *Political Science and Politics,* Spring 1986, *19,* 237–248.

IRIS M. SALTIEL works in a corporate university at Synovus Service Corp., Columbus, Georgia.

*Pursuing formal study as partners can empower, enrich, and help
learners in meaningful ways.*

Adult Students as Partners in Formal Study

Iris M. Saltiel

About fifteen years ago, I observed two adult literacy students working
together. The two were very demanding with each other and gave each other
large homework assignments. They continued to meet and work together. I sat
back in amazement. How could one arrange learners so that they would learn
collaboratively and support one another toward a common goal? That question has remained with me ever since. I've tried to answer it through my work
with adults in different educational programs. In this study, a few more pieces
of the puzzle fell into place. I've learned this much: peer partnerships in learning occur wherever individuals engage in learning pursuits, and these partnerships are filled with magical powers.

   This chapter describes the dynamics that occur between learning partners
who are in pursuit of a formal education credential. It is taken from a larger
study that deals with supports used by adult undergraduate or doctoral students and alumni in home, workplace, and educational environments (Saltiel,
1994). Identified in that study were adult learners who relied on another student to provide mutual support as they completed their degrees. The students
who became involved with other adult learners viewed each other as a central
feature of their larger support systems. They likened their relationships with
each other to a "buddy system" and often attributed their progress and completion to their peers. They identified strongly with these other students who,
like themselves, had familial and work responsibilities and still found a way to
complete their studies. Their interdependence created a safety net—a network
or support system (Mitchell, 1969; Reilly, 1984). Peer-to-peer relationships are
often lauded by students as essential to their completion, yet they are a phenomenon that is rarely, if ever, researched.

NEW DIRECTIONS FOR ADULT AND CONTINUING EDUCATION, no. 79, Fall 1998 © Jossey-Bass Publishers

In this chapter, a learning partner refers to a peer who is pursuing the same educational goal through a formal course of study. Learning partners are different than peer teachers, who are also peers, but teach under the supervision of a teacher (Whitman, 1988). The term "peer tutor" is used when students assist each other on a one-to-one basis (Dueck, 1993).

In their research on informal and incidental learning, Marsick and Watkins (1990) illustrate some ways coworkers learn from one another at the workplace. Employee training and education necessitates that workers inform and assist each other in order to learn what they need for their jobs. A study of health care practitioners conducted by Lovin (1992) showed the importance of partners in informal learning. Lovin detected four types of interactions between partners, and examined partnerships as sources of learning. While partner learning is considered an informal learning strategy, it is often regarded by learners as critical to their success. Many learners seek out a "study buddy" or learning partner as part of establishing and enhancing a support system. These learning partnerships consist of dyads and, on occasion, triads, which provide each of the partners with significant assistance. The ways students utilize peers to enhance learning are distinctive.

Learning Partnerships

A learning partnership is one in which the learners select their partners. Learning partnerships are based on mutual needs, skills, trust, and reciprocity. These attributes complement one another. Members of learning partnerships believe that their relationship empowers them to succeed. Many partners tend to view their contribution as minimal in contrast with what they receive. Their relative strengths and weaknesses are integrated into a working alliance focused on helping each other succeed at the task at hand and look toward the goal. Reflecting on his own experiences, Wildavsky (1986) said, "The feeling that I have gained more than I could possibly give has maintained my interest in collaboration as a vital mode of learning" (p. 239).

Partnerships have many facets. As in any other type of relationship, there are stages of development. The next sections illustrate what happens within the learning partnership when peers pursue formal education together.

Forming a Partnership. There are two ways in which a learning partnership can be formed: intentional and unintentional. In an intentional partnership, the partners already have a relationship when they decide to pursue a common goal together. They know each other and decide to embark on pursuing a degree together as a strategy for getting through. Imel (1994), in her work on using peer tutoring for adult basic education, notes that a "preestablished relationship" provides a strong foundation for working together. Lovin (1992), considering a long-term partnership, characterized the relationship as: "two people acting as one" (p. 64). Students in an intentional partnership will look to one another and say things like, "Three years and out. In three years we'll be done." They talk of assisting one another in their common pursuit of a degree. It is a planned strategy for completion. Their relationship broadens to encompass this new experience. In many intentional partnerships, the first collaborative decision—to carpool with each other—is made without an understanding of how much they will support each other beyond shared transportation.

Unintentional partnerships occur when events happen that bond the individuals together. Inadvertent meetings at registration, similar study or library times, or negotiating similar practical problems might provide enough of an impetus to start the process. The individuals already hold a common goal, and their relationship evolves over time. Making the decision to work together empowers the individuals to move forward. It is an energizing event, similar to the finding of a new job, in which a decision is made and there is a sense of newly found commitment and opportunity for achievement. With the decision behind them, the partners move ahead and discover ways they can support each other.

In many partner relationships, the initial talks are concerned with the logistics of carpooling together. Carpooling provides a regular, routinized time for discussions surrounding a mutual goal. The partners plan to take courses together. The talk centers on completion. The constant reinforcement and dialogue solidifies the goal for each partner.

Working Together. As their interactions continue, the relationship between the learners solidifies and they become partners, very much like a team. Katzenbach and Smith (1993) describe a team as a small group of people with complementary skills committed to a common goal (p. 21). Many partners develop an intuitive understanding of how the other thinks. They begin to anticipate their partner's reactions to the ups and downs of balancing work, family, and education. Slowly and subtly, the changes necessary to promote cooperation occur. The intimacy that develops between learning partners is in itself energizing to the effort. Recollections of a learning partnership often include observations of the value of the relationship separate from the learning content: "We became friendly. Our topics were not similar, but we were each other's support. Moral support was extremely important, and we did that for each other."

The collaborative relationship of learning partners is often characterized by a blending of complementary skills and needs. Through the closely knit involvement with another student, the learner sometimes benefits from characteristics that he or she does not possess. For example, a doctoral student lacked confidence in her ability to pace and organize herself. She purposely sought out another student as a partner in learning because she saw that student as highly organized and efficient. She described the partnership as follows: "Sue would be the one who would keep me on focus. She would call and bounce ideas around that would get me back on track. She set a pace that I struggled to follow." Sue's partner was probably unaware of her value to Sue by providing the context in which Sue could organize her own thoughts through discussion. From another learner: "We needed each other for different things, to see where [we] were." Erikson (cited in Clark and others, 1996) summarized this type of collaboration as, "working together in ways that exchange mutual help" (p. 196).

The mutual involvement and reciprocity associated with a learning partnership provides more than emotional and moral support. It is a structure that provides for regular sharing of ideas and information. Collaborations like this provide members with an in-depth understanding of the work of another person (Clark and others, 1996). The negotiation of practical concerns, such as scheduling assignments and times to meet on a calendar, provide a space for setting goals. Says one student, "We would always do all the problems on our own and then meet and go through the problems and try to find the correct answer."

A defining aspect of a learning partnership is the reciprocity of the relationship—its give-and-take nature. The learning partnership provides for the maintenance of peer status. It is a relationship between equals; what each brings to the relationship is valued as an integral part of the effort toward success. There is an interdependence of the partners' style of operation that is imperative for the administration of practical tasks and for the exchange of ideas. It is the spirit of shared helping that moves both the academics and the relationship along. The nature of the helping depends on the specific skills and resources available. Partners sometimes take turns providing the impetus to keep the other going, while the specific skills or resources of each partner are required throughout the project. The brainstorming of ideas, the reliance on a vehicle suitable for carpooling, or the provision of computer skills or photocopying services are some ways that this give and take is experienced. As one student reflected, "We edited for each other, and at the end of it we were measuring the margins. . . . One person didn't have access to a computer. Didn't know how to use it. Somebody else was going to do it for everybody."

A characteristic of learning enterprises is the ebb and flow of progress. The dynamics of the learning partnership provide a gyroscopic effect, helping the learners stay on course. Scheduling regular meetings and the juxtaposition of the different partner rhythms through the phases of learning has a moderating effect on any tendency to stagnate along the way. As one student recalled, "A lot of those cold Friday nights, one of us didn't want to go; the other two dragged him along." And from another student, "We all set little goals for ourselves. Next week you're gonna write ten pages. So everybody's gonna have ten pages."

It was common for the sharing of progress to spur the other partner to renew their endeavor. The news of another's task completion is often sufficient to prod a partner to overcome his or her own inertia. "She would call and say to me, I finished my paper. And I'm still sitting there with the books. . . . She set a pace."

A variety of practical concerns and predicaments arise in efforts such as these. Partners in learning address these issues as they unfold over the duration of courses. As they gain experience in dealing with these practical matters, they develop a structure and a style that are durable and resilient. Their relationship grows to encompass dealing with the common problems they face in all areas of their lives in general and in adjusting their lives to completing degree work. About handling problems with finding parking in the Lincoln Center area of New York, a carpooling learner recalled, "We'd drive in pairs.

One would sit (behind the wheel) and have to drive it around (laughter). She would try and take orders (from the passenger)." It is often relatively insignificant hurdles, like parking, that will cause a person to drop out.

The structure of study times and routines evolves as a natural outgrowth of partner schedules and their ability to arrive at a harmonious integration of available times and task demands. One alumna spoke of how she arranged her schedule of household errands and chores around the time on Saturday that her study group would meet. Another student described a situation in which he and his learning partner worked for the same company and used their lunch time to meet. Weekends are typically times when adult learners can find time for their study; if partners do not physically meet, they may use weekend telephone calls to discuss ideas, monitor progress, or give and receive emotional support. Here a student describes one such call: "Sunday afternoons she would call me, and say, 'What are you doing?' I'd say, 'Oh, I'm trying to write.' And she'd say, 'Where are you?' And I'd say, 'Well I'm on Chapter Four.' And then she would tell me something that she had done on Chapter Four."

Learning About Themselves. Developing self-awareness and self-empowerment through a learning partnership is similar to participation in other peer support systems. In groups such as Alcoholics Anonymous, Weight Watchers, and cancer recovery groups, developing oneself is the reason for the collaborative effort. In learning partnerships, self-development is not necessarily a part of the original plan, but through immersion in partnership relationships and the feedback they receive from their efforts, learners become more aware of themselves: the roles they occupy, their strengths and weaknesses, their needs, and their wants. Their sense of self-adequacy is altered and established through their involvement in a partnership. They modify their behavior based on their assessment of another learner as a reference point. As one student said, "You're measuring yourself against them." The close nature of the collaboration provides a reference for learners in assessing their own capacities and rhythms of work. This promotes competition between the learners that helps regulate their progress. The comment from one student was, "We did have a sort of camaraderie, and were able to check each other," and, from another student, "There's a little competition, which is good, too."

The learning partners also learn about their ability to participate with and be fueled by another. The relationship becomes important as a place to discharge emotional tension, both from the stress of academic work and from other sources. Students commented, "The partnership became my social activity for two and a half years" and, "We developed a friendship. . . . We're almost letting blood out of ourselves." The awareness of the value they receive from the collaboration serves to ensure that they meet their obligations to their partner. The frequency of meetings, regular contact, and having to negotiate the logistics of going to school as a working adult results in a harmonization of efforts that provide for the development of an intimate relationship. Intimacy also results from the fact that the goal of earning a degree is often closely tied to one's sense of self.

The learning partnership is predisposed to an intensity of emotion that is atypical of other adult relationships. The intimacy that develops is associated with the task involved. No one outside the learning partnership who helps one of the learners can truly comprehend the impact of their help on the learning. Often, only the partner truly understands the nature of the assistance or, for that matter, the obstacle encountered. Only the other partner appreciates and shares in the impact that going to school has on the relationships that predate the involvement with learning. The affirmation of success or the sharing of a setback is central to the intimacy of the learning partnership. The awareness that "Misery loves company. We all shared the same feelings" is common. One student offered a comparison of the partnership to being in the military, "It's almost like in the army, where you had a buddy system."

That the learning partnership ultimately becomes a relationship predicated on friendship, respect, and trust is not surprising. Such an important relationship could not proceed if these attributes were absent. As the relationship continues, the individuals acquire a history of understanding as they mutually participate in each other's lives. Their respect for each other grows as they become more aware of the difficulties that they themselves face and as they witness the other engaged in the effort. Help is supplied in a way that respects the individual being helped: "So while they helped me, they also didn't make me feel helpless." Their strong allegiance to each other develops as they push themselves and each other over obstacles and through assignments. Partners are intensely loyal to each other. They have the basis for shared emotional reactions that none outside the experience can directly know. Participation in the repetitions of the learning activities—the classes, the study group meetings, the telephone calls and carpooling—reinforce the bonds of that experience.

Integrating Intellectual and Personal Aspects. There are many ways that learners help one another toward academic goals. Often their brainstorming provides the foundation for possible research topics, helps one of them reconceptualize a research problem, or even suggests a clever way of managing a situational life dilemma that interferes with coursework. The catalytic assistance they provide for each other is clearly depicted in the comments of one student, who noted, "Hearing an outline that somebody put together helped you to put something else together." The regular monitoring and critical feedback they provide for each other promotes joint progress toward their goal. For one group, carpooling was the arena in which much of this kind of activity would take place: "During that forty minutes we would talk about how we were gonna write a paper. What would you put in yours? Where should we start? How would we go? Where would we go from here?"

The personal growth that accompanies learning is fueled by observations and reflections of progress through the partnership experience. Involvement with learning is heightened by working with another (Chickering and Gamson, 1987). Having a partner along for the journey brings about increased awareness of one's own capabilities and system of working. In the words of one student, "Whenever we took a course together, he was driven to be perfect, had to get the 'A.' And I tend to be the same way. We're both driven by competition. We'd compete with each other, but we'd work toward a common goal."

The partners' experiences, mutual dedication, and common goal reinforces the personal commitment to completion. Using the partner as both guide and role model for envied traits is not uncommon. One student explained, "She was the person who I chose to measure myself to because she seemed to have a straighter path."

Learners in partner relationships often experience a significant personal transformation. The students are more accomplished and secure in their knowledge that they will succeed. They believe in their abilities to produce learning (Imel, 1994).

It is difficult to ascertain what significance working within a partner relationship has on academics. Clark (1993) says understanding learning that is transformational is more complex because of the multiple psychosocial factors (p. 53). Adult students have multiple factors motivating them to earn a degree, ranging from family to work to personal introspective reasons, which results in complexity for those trying to determine critical elements with certainty.

The excitement of learning takes hold as the partnership develops and progress is made, reinforcing the desire to learn and accomplish more. The relationship resonates, intensifying the desire to master the material and keep pace in order to keep up as well as to provide assistance. Learning partners meet the challenge of staying with the material in order to maintain the relationship as well as make progress. Another role a partner assumes is to review the ideas and work of their partner and dare them to think differently. One student said, "We'd go into the office, close the door, and challenge each other."

Perhaps the most valuable role of a partner is the one of helpful critic. It is the strength and depth of the relationship and its foundation of trust and respect permit the constructive criticism that is, perhaps, the ultimate reward of the collaboration. The shared burden, sensitivity, and understanding of the other allows for the productive and nondefensive review of one partner's effort. One student commented, "If someone got off on the wrong path, we were able to pull him back and say, 're-evaluate this,' or 'read this text,' and we did get a grasp of the material and go in the right direction." The provision of this "reality check" is a welcome event, providing both warning and solution in a rather direct manner. As one doctoral alumnus recalled, "We were even meeting when we got back to do rewrites, to read the comments and read the changes so that we could make sure that we were doing the right thing."

Endings. The partnership ends for most of these students when their degrees are earned. Their goal met, the relationship is over. Particularly if the relationship began as an unintentional partnership, the objective is met and the relationship ceases. Partners take away the strong camaraderie of the adventure and will always reflect positively on the experience. If the partnering was intentional, a stronger relationship ensues. These learning partnerships take place within the context of a learning pursuit within the confines of one's life. Regardless of how they began, learners recall the special bonding fondly, recognizing that it was a relationship formed with a purpose and that the purpose is gone.

Closing Thoughts

There are some obvious benefits to learners in a formal course of study who engage in an intentional or unintentional partner relationship. Working with a partner toward a common goal can move partners more effectively and efficiently toward that goal—and often, beyond it. The learning partner provides constant reinforcement and competition while being very supportive. For some, the relationship extends beyond the experience and a real friendship ensues.

A true partnership is an intimate sharing and an open relationship, based on trust and reciprocal give and take without destructive competitive feeling. Learning partnerships are a special kind of student empowering and motivational tool. They rely on collaborative learning. As Chickering and Gamson (1987) said, "Good learning, like good work, is collaborative and social, not competitive and isolated" (p. 4). All learners gain from the experience of working collaboratively and collectively to meet a mutual goal (Clark and others, 1996). Academic programs should be planned to take advantage of peers who are of strong assistance to other students (Whitman, 1988). Educators who facilitate the practice of partnerships for learning give their students a tool for life.

References

Caffarella, R. S. "Self-Directed Learning." In S. B. Merriam (ed.), *An Update on Adult Learning Theory.* New Directions for Adult and Continuing Education, no. 57. San Francisco: Jossey-Bass, 1993.

Chickering, A. W., and Gamson, Z. F. "Seven Principles for Good Practice in Undergraduate Education." *AAHE Bulletin,* 1987, *39* (7), 3–7. (ED 282 491)

Clark, C., Moss, P. A., Goering, S., Herter, R. J., Lamar, B., Leonard, D., Robbins, S., Russell, M., Templin, M., and Wascha, K. "Collaboration as Dialogue: Teachers and Researchers Engaged in Conversation and Professional Development." *American Educational Research Journal,* 1996, *33* (1), 193–231.

Clark, M. C. "Transformational Learning." In S. B. Merriam (ed.), *An Update on Adult Learning Theory.* New Directions for Adult and Continuing Education, no. 57. San Francisco: Jossey-Bass, 1993.

Dueck, G. *Picture Peer Partner Learning: Students Learning from and with Each Other.* Instructional Strategies Series no. 10. Saskatchewan, Canada: Regina University, 1993.

Imel, S. *Peer Tutoring in Adult Basic and Literacy Education.* ERIC Digest No. 146. Columbus: ERIC Clearinghouse on Adult, Career, and Vocational Education, Center on Education and Training for Employment, The Ohio State University, 1994.

Katzenbach, J. R., and Smith, D. K. *The Wisdom of Teams: Creating the High-Performance Organization.* Boston: Harvard Business School Press, 1993.

Lovin, B. K. "Professional Learning Through Workplace Partnerships." In H. K. Morris Baskett and V. J. Marsick (eds.), *Professionals' Ways of Knowing: New Findings on How to Improve Professional Education.* New Directions for Adult and Continuing Education, no. 55. San Francisco: Jossey-Bass, 1992.

Marsick, V. J., and Watkins, K. E. *Informal and Incidental Learning in the Workplace.* New York: Routledge, 1990.

Mitchell, J. C. "The Concept and Use of Social Networks." In J. C. Mitchell (ed.), *Social Networks in Urban Situations: Analyses of Personal Relationships in Central African Towns.* Manchester, England: Manchester University Press, 1969.

Reilly, E. J. "New Dimensions in Learning for Older Adults: Peer Learning Networks for Seniors." Unpublished doctoral dissertation, Teachers College, Columbia University, 1984.

Saltiel, I. M. "Support Systems: A Comparison of Factors That Influence Adult Doctoral and Undergraduate Students Who Are Employed Full Time." Unpublished doctoral dissertation, , Administration, Policy, and Urban Education, Fordham University, 1994.

Whitman, N. A. *Peer Teaching: To Teach Is to Learn Twice.* Association for the Study of Higher Education Report no. 4, 1988, Washington, D.C.

Wildavsky, A. "On Collaboration." *American Political Science Association,* Spring 1986, *19,* 237–248.

IRIS M. SALTIEL works in a corporate university at Synovus Service Corp., Columbus, Georgia.

The kind of partnership formed by teachers and learners in the arts is instructive for those seeking to facilitate learning that leads to new perspectives and paradigms as well as creative solutions to problems.

Teaching-Learning Partnerships in the Arts

Angela Sgroi

> In all this strange time this
> strange woman is my only reality
>   Whoever thought that Sarah Toby
> would be my only reality?
>   All the others are faded away
> and I am in a dance class
>   alone but with Sarah Toby.
> > —Excerpt from "Lazarus," a poem written by
> > an adult dance student about her teacher

This excerpt describes, in part, a learning partnership. Although most students in the arts do not express their sentiments poetically, the intensity of her emotions is not uncommon for those who study in these disciplines. Quite possibly, learning focused on producing original work brings about this kind of passion. It undoubtedly happens in other disciplines as well.

A special kind of partnership forms between teachers in the arts and many of their students. This chapter describes these relationships based on data from two different studies. The first is a study of amateur adult dancers and how they learned modern dance (Sgroi, 1989), and the second consists of preliminary findings on teachers and learners in several art forms (Sgroi, 1997).

Although I do not teach in the arts, I have continued to investigate the way learning, and now teaching, proceeds in these disciplines because I believe that it illuminates for me, and I hope for the teachers in many other disciplines, a kind of teaching and learning that is very much needed. It represents a partnership—which is usually not viewed as a partnership, since it takes place in a group class setting, but it is a partnership, nevertheless. It develops somewhat differently from other partnerships, but it maintains the essential elements. Those elements are included in the following definition of partnership, which will be used in this chapter. A partnership is a self-formed, goal-driven, mutual relationship based on trust and respect, in which both parties believe that they need the other to accomplish mutual goals.

The societal issues we face demand solutions arrived at through entirely new perspectives and paradigms. Where is that process developed and modeled? How can people develop the sense of confidence needed to venture out into uncomfortable, even threatening, new perspectives and paradigms if there is no training ground to practice this way of thinking and working?

A link between thinking in new paradigms and the type of thinking that occurs in the arts is made by Jamake Highwater (1981) in his book, *The Primal Mind*. Highwater attempts to describe and interpret the perspective and experience of primal peoples for the dominant Western-oriented cultures of the United States and most of Europe. He believes that it is in the arts that the two vastly different worldviews overlap. Essentially, his position is that the expanded worldview of a small segment of Western society (artists) is like the normal life experience of primal peoples. He believes, further, that understanding and even emulating the "primal" worldview would bring a better balance to the world. According to Highwater:

> In the broadest sense, the primal mind is a point of departure for a much larger idea. It is a metaphor for a type of otherness that parallels the experience of many people born into the dominant society who feel intensely uncomfortable and alien. . . . There is 'an alien' in all of us. There is an artist in all of us. Of this there is simply no question. The existence of a visionary aspect in every person is the basis for the supreme impact and pervasiveness of art. Art is a staple of humanity. . . . Art is so urgent, so utterly linked with the pulse of feeling in people, that it becomes the singular sign of life when every other aspect of civilization fails: in concentration camps, among the brutalized and the dispossessed, the mad and the too mighty. The people of the caves of Altamira built scaffolds in the dark interiors of their rock caverns. . . . They were spending their time drawing pictures [instead of] . . . finding food . . . to invest the rocks with their story: their myths, their histories, their totems. [pp. 15–16]

If we accept Highwater's notion, when someone is taught to create artwork in Western society, it is likely that they are attaining more than mere skill in craft, they are transformed into individuals with expanded worldviews and, perhaps, greater visionary and creative capabilities in general. It is this type of learning that I discovered in the study of learners of modern dance (Sgroi, 1989). I also discovered, in that study, the critical and specific role of the teacher in nurturing that learning. This discovery was mirrored in the preliminary data on the teachers from the study of teachers and learners in several art forms (Sgroi, 1997).

The purpose of this chapter is to summarize the characteristics of the teacher-learner relationships in these two studies of learning in the arts and to explore some of the ways that Highwater's concepts of "alien" or "visionary" might lead to new ways of seeing and thinking.

The Partnerships

It seems clear from both studies that learning in the arts (and, no doubt, in most other disciplines) is, in fact, a partnership. In the study of dance students, a major factor in their passion for dance and in their success, according to the dancers, was the special relationships they formed with key teachers. They took classes in a certain dance form (jazz, modern, ballet) or at a particular studio *because* of the teacher, often following her or him to new locations. The dance students describe "the good teacher" as someone who has full knowledge of modern dance and teaching dance and is a professional role model; who has high expectations for her or his adult students; and who works with the whole person, inspires trust, and has a powerful influence on dance students (Sgroi, 1989, pp. 107–108).

The dance students were clearly self-directed. Although they did not refer to these relationships with their teachers as partnerships, it began to look as though, in fact, they were partnerships. Using the definition stated earlier, these dancers chose to have a special connection with a specific teacher, so they were self-formed from that point of view. They were goal driven; the dancers respected and trusted their teacher, and the dancers believed they needed their teacher to accomplish their goals.

The modern dance study (Sgroi, 1989) raised some new questions, which were pursued in the follow-up teacher-learner pilot study (Sgroi, 1997): How do the teachers see these relationships? Do such relationships form in the learning that takes place in other art forms? Is there an identifiable pattern or dynamic that develops between teachers and learners in the arts? What can those of us who teach in other disciplines glean from this?

The characteristics of the teaching-learning interaction that emerged from the preliminary data in the teacher-learner study resemble the characteristics of partnerships, even though the teachers interviewed work in classroom situations with groups of students. This happens because of the nature of the learning in the arts: it is time-intensive, and it often requires a great degree of emotional, personal, and intellectual revelation and resources on the part of the learner, and keen observational skills and insight on the part of the teacher. What follows is a summary of the interviews with arts teachers and an interpretation of a learning process that moves learners toward new paradigms and perspectives.

Elements of the Teacher-Learner Dynamic in the Arts

The words of an art teacher provide a succinct overview of the elements of the teacher-learner dynamic: "So as a teacher that was to be my part: not to tell them, but to sort of help them open some doors, allow them to see, also give them the confidence—and that's a very big part of my teaching. There is some kind of trust and faith established. I don't know how it happens exactly. People have told me time and again—the kids themselves. They will go anywhere with me. Why that is, I don't know."

The first element of the dynamic is developing trust; then comes the task of acquiring the tools needed to navigate the unknown territory through which every artist must travel in order to create original artwork. The third and fourth elements are the roles of the teachers and the roles of the learners in the partnership.

Developing Trust. Daloz (1986) uses the metaphor of a journey into the unknown in his book *Effective Teaching and Mentoring: Realizing the Transformational Power of Adult Learning Experiences.* The metaphor provides a useful image for describing the patterns that have emerged in the initial phase of the 1997 study. For the learner, the journey is essentially a journey inward. The only vehicle on which the journey can be made is trust: the journey cannot be made unless the learner trusts the guide, but also the learner must trust herself or himself.

The trust described by the art teacher in the preceding quote is echoed by one of the adult dancers: "You are their clay. . . . It's the ultimate romantic sort of teacher-pupil relationship because you work for them. You try, you just try. . . ." (Sgroi, 1989, p. 105). A theater teacher explains that students trust her because she gives them "things that they know are going to make them good."

As in most human relationships, trust is the bedrock. Without it, no relationship exists. With it, people are transformed. Each of the tools needed to negotiate the unknown—seeing, risk taking, removing barriers, expanding the palette, finding the daemon, working, connecting, and conducting self-critiques—are basic teaching objectives used by many teachers in different situations. What makes them powerful tools for the often difficult and sometimes frightening unknown of the artist is their basis in a deeply trusting relationship. Therefore, each teacher to some extent needs to have a one-on-one relationship with each student, even in class settings.

Tools Needed to Negotiate the Unknown. Trust gives the partnership the foundation it needs to move ahead into new domains. Then the tools can be developed and the learner can move further into new territory.

Seeing. Each teacher uses techniques that require or lead students to "see" (or hear or read) in new ways. They consistently and intentionally guide the students to observe the work of others, to view materials and techniques in new ways, and to perceive their environment and lives differently. Exposing students to a wide range of art and talking about it, and expecting them to approach their tools and materials in completely new ways are a couple of the approaches used by these teachers to help students see in new ways. For example, a visual artist explains, "I felt the students had to understand what their options were [when working with fibers]. And what they thought something evoked. . . what a knitted surface might evoke as opposed to a hard woven surface. . . . You make the choices. . . . It's your tool, it's your voice. . . . My role as a teacher was somehow to expose them to something besides baby clothes."

Risk Taking. "No risk, no art," announced an art teacher. She added, "You can fall on your face. It's scary as hell and in the visual arts, your failure is tangible. . . . It looks back at you and it's ugly." They may push or pull, or just gently encourage, but the teachers all know that their job is to continually get the learner to move into new territory, to try new ideas and new ways to express them. That is the essence of what they are trying to do. The voice teacher concludes, "Some things can be taught, some things are natural, some things can be unlocked. I would say that there is, to some extent, . . . a performer in everybody."

Risk taking is an obvious and critical tool in creating anything. In writing, the teacher sees her role in guiding her students toward risk in this way: "It seems to me that when anybody sits down with a blank sheet of paper, . . . they don't know what's going to happen. . . . And half the time you fail. . . . I tell them it's sort of like jumping off a cliff and sometimes there's water down there, . . . you can just swim off; and sometimes it's so cold, it catches your breath and you just stop; and sometimes you hit rocks. Creative writing is . . . always a challenge, a risk, and you don't know what's going to happen."

Removing Barriers. Adults, by the time they come to learn to create art, even those who have done it most of their lives, inevitably bring some form of barrier: fears, cultural taboos, or old ways of seeing, knowing, and doing things. These are consciously targeted by the teacher and removed whenever possible.

Numerous techniques to create a feeling of comfort are employed. One theater teacher uses props and costumes to create the environment for imaginative work, and an art teacher uses a lot of collaborative projects. But creating a comfortable environment does not guarantee the student comfort in all things; it may just give the teacher the springboard from which to launch the student's work into uncomfortable new areas. One teacher describes the process this way: "Everybody brings their own sort of baggage. . . . They bring their own ideas and background with them, and sometimes we get locked into that . . . how can you make people sort of expand? That's a big part of teaching. How do you take this person, take them somewhere else? And make them give up some of those walls? I'm doing it constantly. . . . Usually, I tell them I want them to do it just totally opposite of what's comfortable. Because then they'll have to explore new territory."

What these teachers are describing is a continual struggle, because their students want to do things they can control. But the job of the teacher is to force them away from the familiar, to put them in new situations that are uncomfortable, to push them to form new models in their minds.

Expanding the Palette. The palette represents the spectrum of colors, the raw material that learners take with them when they venture into new emotional or creative territory, including a strong foundation in the techniques of the art form, new technical options, and practice in venturing out in protected ways. The writing teacher uses four strategic techniques to both remove the barriers in students' minds and release new writing patterns and ideas. The voice teacher uses theater games, and students perform for one another, first performing a piece as written, then changing the setting or the historic period "so they can put a different perspective on it. And always when you've stretched anything in another direction, when you come back to home, you've got more colors, you've got more possibilities in your interpretations."

Finding the Daemon. Finding the daemon is something all of the arts teachers understand must happen with a learner if anything personally expressive (not necessarily creative, although the two are closely linked) is to happen. The term *daemon* is borrowed from Aristotle, following Waterman (1990), to represent the individuality and essential character of each person. "I want this work to be personal . . . your point of view, your opinion, your *something,*" says an art teacher. A writing teacher comments, "You don't really teach anybody anything. What you do is reveal to them what their real love is." It is something that the learner may not be able to see.

In the arts, these observations and communications lend themselves to nonverbal media. One art teacher talks about a student who, when given the assignment to paint "one important event in your life," made a very garish, clumsy painting of a rock star who had recently committed suicide: "It was everything you can think of in an amateurish portrait. And lurking around in the background was some very wonderful brushwork. I chose not to talk about his ghastly yellow hair, his poorly painted eyes; I chose to look at . . . some of the stuff here that had life. . . . By the end of the semester, this student made the most exciting work."

Working. Hard work, and lots of it, is the basic underlying factor that leads to development of technical skill, creative thinking, and aesthetic sensibility. The learners "need to know . . . that you make a mountain of stuff, and in the mountain, there are a couple of [jewels] . . . and you celebrate." One art teacher comments, "I think any creative discipline, the one thing you have to learn right off . . . it doesn't necessarily make you the best, but the best do it . . . is to work hard." And for writing, one teacher says, "the writing itself engenders writing." Writers write, painters paint, singers sing. Their lives center on that.

Connecting. Teachers connect their students to others in their art form, directly and indirectly. They do it primarily by putting student in touch with student so they can work together; by sending students off to see, hear, or read the work of master artists in the art form; and by modeling their own professional network. Connections with peers and with masters in the field set in motion a lifelong process that yields critiques of works, emotional and intellectual support, and a resource for ideas.

Conducting Self-Critiques. "I think, in terms of their total progress in creative writing, . . . that what they learn is not necessarily to become better writers right away, but to become better critics. And they learn to be able to distance themselves from their work, so that they can stand back and look at it and begin to see themselves," states one teacher. Most of the teachers interviewed use some form of peer feedback to develop students' ability to do good self-critiques. Whatever the technique, the goal is to guide students to critically evaluate their own work.

Role of the Teacher in the Partnership. The role of the teacher includes identifying their relationship with the learner as a partnership even when teaching a group; seeing and describing herself or himself as a guide to learning; cultivating an aesthetic sensibility; modeling the lifestyle; providing a safe haven, and launching the protégé.

Identifying a Partnership. First of all, that these teachers see their relationships with their students as partnerships, even though they primarily teach group classes, is undeniable. Comments like this were common: "A teacher to one extent or another, falls in love with a class, and if you don't it's bad. So, I think there's a real emotional connection with all the students and definitely, especially in writing, because you get to know so much about who they are, what's going on in their head. . . . I feel pretty connected with the students. And everyone for different reasons, so they all seem very individual to me."

This feeling of connection is not surprising, because the teacher-learner connection in the arts, by necessity, is often deeper and more emotionally personal than in other traditional formal teaching settings. The nature of the work forces a degree of intimacy. All the teachers made some sort of reference to the intense one-on-one relationships they have with most of their students.

Guides to Learning. The teachers usually refer to themselves as guides, and each is very specific and articulate about the skills and knowledge they give their students to help them negotiate the unknown and negotiate it without fear. They have clearly identified what is important to learn, breaking it down, making it concrete, creating workable limits.

Cultivating an Aesthetic Sensibility. An art teacher addresses this directly and articulately: "I think aesthetic acuity is very much like taste; it is something that grows slowly and is nurtured. You can't impose it on someone. They must come by it in the natural way. So if a kid reads trash, . . . I would not discourage it, not for an instant. . . . If you read enough of it, it's so tiresome, it's boring. The good stuff isn't boring. And little by little this drops out of your repertoire. You start reaching for something else. . . . And I have all the faith in the human intellect. I have the same faith in my students that, in time, with support, not denigration, they will, in fact, begin to refine their judgments."

Modeling the Lifestyle. Modeling the lifestyle of an artist is a responsibility the teachers recognize and embrace. What they teach is not done just in the classroom. The dance students from the 1989 (Sgroi) study made similar observations about their good teachers. A thirty-eight-year-old amateur dancer offered: "I think they also bring with them, being a professional dancer, a whole ambiance about an experience that we don't have. They can tell stories about this dancer and that dancer. And I think that adds to the whole feeling of the class. They always treated the classes in a professional way. So even though we're not going to a New York stage they still would give you the same class as they would give other people, so I respect them for doing that because I think it makes us a lot better dancers."

Providing a Safe Haven. Teachers' role in providing a safe environment has been discussed in earlier sections of the chapter. This role, for many of these teachers, continues after the students leave their formal instruction. A theater teacher describes hearing from students on and off for as many as fifteen years after having them in a class. She even speculates about why she still hears from so many of her students: "It's almost parental, but it's safe parental. Because there's no judgment involved. I don't have an emotional stake in what they do."

Launching. Ultimately the teacher's goal is to send her or his students off to work on their own, to find their own way. As the voice teacher puts it, "The real test, though, is whether they can go beyond you."

Pushing students to evaluate their own work is the preparation for letting them go. The art teacher explains that her job is to take the scary unknown one faces when looking at a large white canvas and to create a framework and limits within which a particular project must go. She says that it is when students can do this for themselves that they are ready to move on.

Role of the Learner in the Partnership. This is a partnership because the student must contribute as much to the equation as the teacher if any learning is to take place. That is the expectation. Students contribute from a different angle: fresh perspectives, new ideas, critical thinking, new interests and directions. The learner's role includes taking full responsibility for his or her learning; engaging (and engaging the teacher, when necessary) in mutual goal setting; obtaining the attention, care, and guidance needed from the teacher; participating, in a reasonable way, in structuring the learning; interacting with individuals and groups; giving appropriate feedback; working; contributing to the development of mutual loyalty and trust; and being open to receiving new information and ideas or to trying new approaches.

Adapting the Model in Other Fields of Study

One way or the other, all teaching and learning is a partnership between the teacher and the learner. If it is not, learning is not likely to take place. Teachers need to continually be mindful of this. Teaching with the premise that the teacher and learner must work together in some way to accomplish mutually agreed-upon learning goals requires the types of approaches outlined above.

The kind of partnerships that often form between teachers and learners in the arts can provide a model for discovery and development of new realities and new paradigms in any field. I see these models as partnerships that share many of the characteristics Daloz (1986) offers for mentorship. The distinction between his notion of mentor and the arts partnerships described in this chapter may illuminate aspects of partnership that can be useful in other disciplines.

Daloz's broader concept of mentor defines it as a guide on a journey toward truth and transformation; he describes the prototypical mentor as "engendering trust, issuing a challenge, providing encouragement, and offering a vision for the journey" (1986, pp. 29–30). The guide, however, knows the territory where the neophyte is headed: "[The mentor] knows the territory. He is Mentor Supreme, alternately protecting his charge from threat, urging him on, explaining the mysteries, pointing the way, leaving him alone, translating arcane codes, calming marauding beasts, clearing away obstacles, and encouraging—always encouraging" (p. 28).

Teachers in the arts are necessarily, because of the nature of the learning, also guides on the journey. The difference in this type of relationship, however, is that they are guiding someone through territory which is unknown to them as well. They are bringing students into the great unknown, the world Jamake Highwater calls the world of the "other." Because the territory in this field is individual and internal, the teachers usually do not know the arcane codes; they have not faced every marauding beast or encountered every obstacle. Many mysteries must remain unexplained and simply accepted.

Teachers are guides because they have journeyed into this unknown many times themselves and what they do know are the best ways to negotiate the unknown: how to break it down, how to face it, how to find the way, how to live with unexplained mysteries, how to approach and try to translate arcane codes, ways to calm marauding beasts or clear away obstacles.

The way they help learners to negotiate that unknown provides a useful guide for helping to guide anyone who is approaching what Highwater refers to as "otherness"—a vision or reality that is so different than that which the person has known that it is frightening and even unapproachable. Arts educators and some psychologists have argued this for a long time; it is not a new idea. Maslow (1968) wrote, "Creative art education . . . may be especially important not so much for turning out artists or art products, as for turning out better people . . . who are able confidently to face tomorrow not knowing . . . what will happen, with confidence enough in [them]selves that [they] will be able to improvise in that situation which has never existed before" (p. 4).

If we as teachers are concerned about guiding learning toward the kinds of fresh perspectives and new paradigms needed to face the present and emerging challenges of our world, perhaps the teacher-learner patterns described in this chapter can offer inspiration and direction.

References

Daloz, L. A. *Effective Teaching and Mentoring: Realizing the Transformational Power of Adult Learning Experiences.* San Francisco: Jossey-Bass, 1986.

Highwater, J. *The Primal Mind: Vision and Reality in Indian America.* New York: Penguin Books, 1981.

Maslow, A. H. *Toward a Psychology of Being.* (2nd ed.) New York: Van Nostrand Reinhold, 1968.

Sgroi, A. "Adult Amateur Dancers: A Field Study of Their Learning." Unpublished doctoral dissertation, Department of Educational Administration, Supervision, and Adult Education. Rutgers, The State University of New Jersey, 1989.

Sgroi, A. "Interviews with Teachers of the Arts." Unpublished pilot study, Trenton, N.J., 1997.

Waterman, A. S. "Personal Expressiveness: Philosophical and Psychological Foundations." *Journal of Mind and Behavior,* 1990, *11* (1), 47–74.

ANGELA SGROI is executive assistant to the vice president for academic affairs at The College of New Jersey, working primarily to support faculty research and teaching.

This chapter explores the collaborative learning partnership between science fiction writer Robert A. Heinlein and his wife, Virginia Heinlein, in which Virginia's learning projects complemented and enabled Robert's novels and stories.

Silent Partner: The Power Behind the Throne

Phillip H. Owenby

Many science fiction readers (and some adult educators among them) know that Robert Anson Heinlein (1907–1988) used his science fiction as a tool for educating his (mostly adult) readers. However, fewer of those readers know that many ideas that went into his stories originated in his wife Virginia Gerstenfeld Heinlein's many and varied learning projects. Robert said of her, "I'm married to a woman who knows more . . . than I do. . . . Her brain is a great help to me professionally" (Heinlein, 1980a, p. 520). Virginia's partnering also included serving as the model for several self-directed learners in Robert's science fiction.

In this chapter I intend to explore a specific kind of learning partnership—the silent partnership—in which one partner's learning projects complement and enable the activities of the other, more visible partner. Specifically, I will focus on the learning partnership between science fiction writer Robert Heinlein and his wife, Virginia. I wish particularly to deal with those aspects of the Heinleins' partnership that made it successful as a learning-writing-teaching team. By way of positioning the Heinlein's partnership, I will briefly describe a few other writing partnerships—silent and not so silent—that share similarities with the Heinleins'. I will also discuss the history of the Heinleins' partnership to give some necessary background to readers unfamiliar with Robert Heinlein's work. However, the largest portion of this chapter will be devoted to discussing various dimensions of Virginia Heinlein's silent partnership with Robert.

Silent and Not-So-Silent Learning Partnerships Among Writers

Learning partnerships are not unusual among writers. But what is distinctive about many learning partnerships that involve writers is that quite often the writing reflects the learning and teaching interests of the partners. This is especially true of writers whose works—whether fiction or nonfiction—function as vehicles for popular education. For example, one of the well-known American writing partnerships of this century was that of philosophical historians Will and Ariel Durant, who during their life together jointly researched and wrote a massive history of human civilization (Durant and Durant, 1935–1967).

Similarly, science fiction and fantasy writer and popular educator L. Sprague de Camp has had a silent partnership of learning and writing with his wife, Catherine Crook (who edited his books and recently began coauthoring books with him). He also had a partnership with fellow science fiction writer Fletcher Pratt (who, when alive, was not a silent partner). A distinctive feature of their fiction is the large amount of scholarship used to create their plausible and coherent backgrounds. Readers of their works come away highly informed as well as entertained. For example, in *The Compleat Enchanter,* de Camp and Pratt (1975) introduced their readers to psychology, symbolic logic, Norse mythology, Irish history, Spenserian poetry, medieval manners, Islamic culture, Italian epic poetry, Greek mythology, and the legends of Charlemagne.

In Europe, Rudolf Steiner (1951), the Austrian philosopher and founder of the worldwide Waldorf education movement, had a silent learning partner in his wife, Marie. A gifted artist and dancer, Marie not only partnered with her husband as an editor of his publications, but she was also instrumental in developing the unique art form called *eurythmy.* Also called the art of visible speech, eurythmy combines dance and speech to teach children and adults an integrated perspective of mind and body. (For a perspective on the total Waldorf curriculum, see Stockmeyer, 1969.)

Jean-Paul Sartre and Simone de Beauvoir are an example of a learning partnership in which a peer relationship seems to have been absent. This is in spite of the fact that de Beauvoir's work was easily as intellectually impressive as her more famous companion's. Paul Johnson (1988) clearly pointed out the combination of dependence and disrespect that characterized Sartre's relationship with de Beauvoir. Fortunately, the history of Virginia Heinlein's life with Robert Heinlein shows a genuine mutual respect in their silent learning partnership.

In March 1994 I was permitted to visit Virginia as a guest at her home in Florida. There, over a four-day period, I interviewed her on audiotape and was allowed to read and examine personal items and unpublished documents. Much of what follows was taken from twelve hours of recorded interviews (Virginia Heinlein, interviews with the author, March 11–12, 1994) and from Virginia's edited collection of the Heinleins' personal correspondence (Heinlein, 1989).

A Brief History of the Heinlein Partnership

I would describe Robert Heinlein as a science fiction writer who used his science fiction as a platform for popular education. From the time he started writing in 1939, he was concerned with educating his audience about the technological and sociological trends that were dramatically affecting the development of human societies. A former naval officer (Annapolis-trained), engineer, and amateur astronomer, Robert was medically unfit to return to active service when World War II began. Instead he found work as a research and development engineer at Mustin Field, the Navy Air Experiment Center, near Philadelphia. There he worked with two other science fiction writers whom he had recruited for war-related research and development work, Isaac Asimov and L. Sprague de Camp. It was also there that he met Virginia Gerstenfeld in 1944.

Virginia was a twenty-six-year-old junior navy officer (WAVE) when she was assigned to Mustin Field to work as a chemist and aeronautical engineer. A native of Brooklyn, she had graduated from New York University, where she earned varsity letters in several sports as well as a degree in chemistry. After seeing Olympic figure skater Sonja Henie perform in New York, Virginia became an avid figure skater herself. Prior to the war, she worked as a quality control chemist for a large bakery. After the war began, Virginia joined the navy as an officer candidate. Her scientific training made her a natural choice to work in a navy research and development laboratory.

Robert worked with Virginia on various projects, including one—an aircraft Plexiglas project—in which she was the project leader. When the war ended in August 1945, Robert returned with his then wife Leslyn to their prewar home in Hollywood, California. Virginia meanwhile entered UCLA graduate school to study for a master's degree in biochemistry. After Robert's marriage ended in 1947, he sought out Virginia and married her in 1948.

Thus began their learning partnership. During the next forty years, Robert—with the behind-the-scenes support of Virginia—would publish a raft of novels and short stories. Their efforts would result in four Hugo Awards (science fiction's top literary honor), a Grand Master Nebula Award from fellow science fiction writers, and the first science fiction novel ever to make the *New York Times* Best Seller list (*Stranger in a Strange Land*) (Heinlein, [1961] 1987). What were the dimensions of this partnership that made it so successful?

Dimensions of Virginia's Silent Learning Partnership

From the beginning of their marriage in 1948 until Robert's death in 1988, Virginia was a partner in Robert's writing projects as well as his wife and companion. Her contributions as a partner began in small but important ways and gradually increased until it was unthinkable for him to work in any other way. The full scale of her involvement in her husband's work would not be known until after his death.

Her involvement as a partner spanned several dimensions. These included problem solving and researching; monitoring and editing writing projects; engaging in self-directed learning partnerships; serving as a model for self-directed learner characters in Robert's books; facilitating and guiding Robert's attention to learning needs and issues; and managing her husband's lifestyle and health. One of the first contributions Virginia made as a learning partner was in the role of problem solver and researcher.

Problem Solving and Researching. Virginia did not wait long to begin contributing to the learning partnership. The first year they were married, Robert published *Space Cadet* (Heinlein, 1948), a novel describing space flight in scientifically possible terms. To ensure the authenticity of the novel, Virginia helped Robert by painstakingly making ballistic calculations of spacecraft orbits on yards of butcher paper—a necessary chore in the pre–handheld calculator age. These calculations took two days, but they helped ensure the accuracy of a paragraph-long description of a rocket ship flight from Colorado Springs to an orbiting space station.

Virginia's help was not limited to mathematics. After all, she was a trained scientist in the chemical and biological sciences. It was for her expertise in these disciplines that Robert called on her again when he wrote a novel about future human colonization of Ganymede, a planet-sized moon of Jupiter (*Farmer in the Sky*) (Heinlein, 1949). In the novel, humans have learned to "terranize" dead planets by installing earth flora and fauna after converting their rocky surfaces into living soil. Virginia researched the problem of creating soil and wrote a scientific paper on the subject; Robert used the paper as the basis for his technical discussion of the matter in the novel.

Virginia was skilled at philosophical insights as well. For example, in Robert's short story "Gulf" (Heinlein, [1949] 1953), he struggled with a way of conceptualizing the next stage of human evolution; he called this stage "homo novis." When he asked Virginia to consider the characteristic that would most define the new type of human, she answered that it would be the ability to "think better" (p. 46). Robert then immediately knew how to construct his story.

Robert's confidence in his wife's research and problem-solving skills was so firmly established that he unhesitatingly asked her to solve technical problems never before tackled. For example, in writing *Have Space Suit—Will Travel* (Heinlein, 1958), he needed to know the volume of air contained in a space suit. Virginia went to work calculating the unusual dimensions of the hypothetical piece of equipment. When she arrived at the figure, Robert was driven to check her calculations because they were based on figures that disagreed with a standard engineering handbook. As a result, Robert made a pen and ink correction to the handbook's tables; Virginia was right as usual.

Virginia was not above providing research answers to Robert that were full of tongue-in-cheek humor. For example, in *Friday* (Heinlein, 1982), Robert described an environmentalist group protesting for the preservation of an endangered species, and he needed an appropriate candidate. Virginia obligingly suggested *Rhus Diversiloba*—poison oak—for the fictional scenario. Virginia told me that almost nobody who read the novel caught the joke. But Virginia was to have even greater involvement in her husband's books.

Monitoring and Editing Writing Projects. From the beginning Virginia exercised quality control over Robert's books. This role started with *Space Cadet* (Heinlein, 1948), a novel that explores the educational requirements for a future transnational peace enforcement organization. As Virginia remembered, Robert's descriptions of the novel's educational scenes were too lengthy: "When Robert was writing *Space Cadet,* there was one scene between Matt and his teacher, his don, really, in the British sense of the word. He went on and on there, and I made him cut it before he even sent it in . . . because Robert was really being preacherish. The original version just went on and on until you got bleary-eyed over it" (Virginia Heinlein, interviews with the author, March 11–12, 1994).

Similarly, Virginia would caution Robert when he became overly enthusiastic about one of his hobbyhorses. For example, Robert was a devotee of Alfred Korzybski (1941), the founder of general semantics and a proponent of the idea of "mathematicizing" human knowledge. Virginia was able to convince Robert that the idea simply would not always work in practice. Virginia was also able to coach Robert in areas in which he lacked the necessary training. One such area was chemistry, Virginia's specialty. Robert would consequently pass every story idea through Virginia if it involved chemistry.

But Virginia also reported that Robert was able to convince her that other approaches to chemistry were possible even if they were not the commonly accepted ones. That he was able to do so illustrates that Virginia and Robert's learning partnership was not one-sided. In fact, Robert influenced several of Virginia's learning projects.

Self-Directed Learning Projects. Besides the fact that Robert would ask Virginia to take on problem-solving or research projects to aid him in the writing of his books, his suggestions often prompted her to undertake learning projects on her own behalf. For example, she undertook a self-directed learning project in Biblical criticism, reading the works of Albert Schweitzer and especially the essays of Thomas Huxley. She recalled, "Poor Robert didn't get fed anything until I finished reading those. But Robert led me into that study, so I can't exactly blame myself entirely" (Virginia Heinlein, interviews with the author, March 11–12, 1994).

Virginia was also led into the study of computers and programming after Robert decided to exchange his typewriter for one of the first word-processing computers. Impatient with the machine's quirks, Robert would rely on Virginia to troubleshoot hardware and software problems so that he could get back to work. She described her learning project this way: "I worked for a couple of years on computers. When we began to use computers there weren't any intelligible books on the subject, and I just figured out for myself how it worked, and I studied. I subscribed to all [the periodicals] and I got every book I could find on the subject of computers and so forth. And I really did learn quite a bit about them. And then I decided, 'Look, this thing is just a tool and I am not a programmer by nature, so I think I'll drop this study and just use it as such' " (Virginia Heinlein, interviews with the author, March 11–12, 1994).

Robert eventually realized that he was overly dependent on Virginia's computer knowledge. She recalled that he "would get into a mess with his computer [and] call me in and say, 'Tell me how to do it.' So, I would stand there and watch over his shoulder and tell him what to do, and he would do it, and he would get the answer that he wanted" (Virginia Heinlein, interviews with the author, March 11–12, 1994).

Both Virginia and Robert were interested in languages, and their mutual interest spurred their continual learning. So also did their practical needs. For example, in 1960 Robert and Virginia visited the length and breadth of the Soviet Union. For two years prior to their trip Virginia studied Russian, taking extension courses from the local university and buying every Russian self-study course available. She kept Russian language records "stacked on the record changer and played them all day long while she did other things—our home had a speaker in every room" (Heinlein, 1980b, pp. 403–404). By the time the Heinleins visited the Soviet Union, Virginia could read, write, speak, and think in Russian. Virginia's hard work enabled them to learn far more from their trip than otherwise would have been possible. Virginia ultimately learned to speak, read, and write seven languages. There is little wonder that Robert modeled self-directed characters in his novels after Virginia.

Role Modeling for Self-Directed Learner Characters. Virginia related to me that she "could see bits and pieces" of herself in almost every story Robert wrote (Virginia Heinlein, interviews with the author, March 11–12, 1994). But some of Robert's self-directed characters were clearly more influenced by Virginia than others. For example, the juvenile character Betty Sorenson in *The Star Beast* (Heinlein, 1954) is responsible for figuring out the legal and personal difficulties of the protagonist. Similarly, the character Vicky in *Time for the Stars* (Heinlein, 1956) asserts herself to become a special communicator in order to enable the protagonist to communicate from light years away.

Virginia also served as the model for the precocious children in Robert's stories. One of the most memorable is Patricia Reisfeld—called Pee Wee—in *Have Space Suit—Will Travel* (Heinlein, 1958). Pee Wee is modeled after Virginia in almost all respects, even in the way that her last name shares similar German associations ("Reisfeld" means rice field; "Gerstenfeld"—Virginia's maiden name—means barley field). But Virginia's qualities are especially evident in Pee Wee's self-directed approach to learning, her curiosity, and her ability to create novel solutions to problems.

Robert also modeled his first woman protagonist after Virginia (Heinlein, 1982). The protagonist is a high-security commercial courier who is athletic, brilliant, curious, and resourceful—all characteristics of Virginia's as well. Friday is also one of the most able self-directed learners of any in Robert's stories, and she is used by her employer in the same way that Robert used Virginia—

to answer difficult questions about complex subjects. In addition to that role, Virginia also actively guided Robert in regard to what he attended to and learned.

Managing Robert's Learning, Entertainment, and Health. Virginia took an active role in deciding what Robert should read and how he should be kept informed. Some of her choices were made to please Robert. For example, she knew he enjoyed Mark Twain, so she set about acquiring a complete set of Twain's books and short stories, including stories that had gone out of print. Robert's allusions to these lesser-known works have inspired many readers to undertake frustrated literary searches for out-of-print Twainiana.

Besides the works of Mark Twain, Virginia also ensured that Robert had access to first-rate reference books and periodicals. For example, she bought three separate editions of the *Encyclopaedia Britannica* and installed them over his workspace. In addition, she acquired numerous mathematics, technical, and scientific source books so that Robert could have ready access to formulas, figures, and tables to inform his writing. Virginia also initiated and maintained subscriptions and society memberships in order to ensure a steady flow of scientific and engineering literature into their household. Eventually, the Heinleins would accumulate over ten thousand books in their home library.

Virginia would also serve as Robert's director of entertainment. For example, she would select or influence the acquisition of music recordings and art books. In addition, during their trips to New York to visit agents and publishers, Virginia would investigate the Broadway offerings and select their entertainment fare. During one such visit, Robert insisted on seeing the Broadway offering of *The Caine Mutiny Court Martial*. But he had been led into his interest in that play by Virginia's urging him to read the book by Herman Wouk much earlier.

Virginia was largely responsible for planning and managing their regular travels, both at home and abroad. I have already mentioned their trip to the Soviet Union, but Virginia made a point of being well researched and tutored for virtually every trip the Heinleins took. This included reading articles and books in preparation for each trip as well as acquiring native publications and other information sources once they arrived at their destination. After returning home from each trip, Virginia would write a report of their travels and file it away. Robert would use Virginia's travel reports to recall details of languages and customs in order to flesh out his novels.

Finally, Virginia managed Robert's lifestyle and health. For example, she protected his time so that he could write without distractions. She reorganized his research and business files by creating a numbering system that resembled a relational database in operation—but in paper form. Virginia managed Robert's business affairs and correspondence with agents, publishers, writers, and fans. And she monitored Robert's health, ensuring that he received enough rest, food, recreation, and—during his frequent illnesses—medical and nursing care. In fact, Robert declared that Virginia had added at least ten years to his life through her care and attention (Heinlein, 1980c, p. 456).

Problems and Limitations. Not all was rosy in regard to Virginia's silent learning partnership with Robert. Certainly it must have been limiting for Virginia to organize her entire life around her husband's novels. "Had I not been so involved in helping Robert," said Virginia, "I would likely have spent more time learning about my personal interests. Still, it was a good life. I was seldom bored" (personal communication with Virginia Heinlein, September 21, 1996).

Also time-consuming was the burden of being Robert's business manager. And because their learning partnership was also a marriage, difficulties in one area of their shared lives had a way of affecting other areas as well. Virginia recalled that "just like in all marriages, tensions would build up and we would have quite a little row" (personal communication with Virginia Heinlein, September 21, 1996). Perhaps what made both areas of their relationship a success was their mutual emotional and intellectual trust. I have already mentioned the tribute that Robert made to his wife (Heinlein, 1980c, p. 456). Her tribute is indicated by these words: "Robert spoiled me for other people. I never knew anyone else like him" (personal communication with Virginia Heinlein, March 11, 1994).

Conclusion

At the beginning of this chapter I set out to explore a specific kind of learning partnership—the silent learning partnership between science fiction writer Robert Heinlein and his wife Virginia. I have described various dimensions of their partnership. But the overriding characteristic of their learning partnership—running through all the dimensions—is that Virginia's silent role complemented and enabled the activities of Robert, her more visible partner.

Robert and Virginia Heinlein were partners in learning who helped each other see what they would never have seen on their own. The Heinleins exhibited characteristics of mutual support, empowerment, and a complementary yet reciprocal peer relationship. The marriage relationship of Virginia and Robert seems to have enabled some aspects of their learning partnership. This appears to be especially true in regard to how trust, love, and shared experiences support and enable mutual learning. In recognition of this, I am glad to be able to help give voice to Virginia's long, silent learning partnership with Robert A. Heinlein.

References

de Camp, L. S., and Pratt, F. *The Compleat Enchanter.* New York: Del Rey Books, 1975.

Durant, W., and Durant, A. *The Story of Civilization.* 10 vols. New York: Simon & Schuster, 1935–1967.

Heinlein, R. A. *Space Cadet.* New York: Scribner, 1948.

Heinlein, R. A. *Farmer in the Sky.* New York: Scribner, 1949.

Heinlein, R. A. "Gulf." In *Assignment in Eternity.* New York: Signet Books, 1953. (Originally published 1949.)

Heinlein, R. A. *The Star Beast.* New York: Scribner, 1954.

Heinlein, R. A. *Time for the Stars.* New York: Ace Books, 1956.

Heinlein, R. A. *Have Space Suit—Will Travel.* New York: Scribner, 1958.

Heinlein, R. A. "The Happy Days Ahead." In *Expanded Universe.* New York: Ace Books, 1980a.

Heinlein, R. A. "'Pravda' Means 'Truth.'" In *Expanded Universe.* New York: Ace Books, 1980b.

Heinlein, R. A. "Searchlight." In *Expanded Universe.* New York: Ace Books, 1980c.

Heinlein, R. A. *Friday.* New York: Del Rey Books, 1982.

Heinlein, R. A. *Stranger in a Strange Land.* New York: Ace Books, 1987. (Originally published 1961.)

Heinlein, R. A. *Grumbles from the Grave.* (V. Heinlein, ed.) New York: Del Rey Books, 1989.

Johnson, P. "Jean-Paul Sartre: 'A Little Ball of Fur and Ink.'" In *Intellectuals.* New York: HarperCollins, 1988.

Korzybski, A. *Science and Sanity.* (2nd ed.) Lancaster, Pa.: Science Press Printing, 1941.

Steiner, R. *The Course of My Life* (O. D. Wannamaker, trans.). Bell's Pond, Hudson, N.Y.: Anthroposophic Press, 1951.

Stockmeyer, E.A.K. *Rudolf Steiner's Curriculum for Waldorf Schools* (R. Everett-Zade, trans.). Forest Row, England: Steiner Schools Fellowship, 1969.

Phillip H. Owenby coordinates executive, strategic, and technology-assisted learning programs for TVA University, the corporate learning institute of the Tennessee Valley Authority in Knoxville, Tennessee.

When a mentoring relationship evolves into a partnership, new potentials for synergy and mutual growth become possible.

From Mentor to Partner: Lessons from a Personal Journey

Roger Hiemstra, Ralph G. Brockett

In recent years, the literature on mentoring has exploded. In the adult education field alone, several major publications have addressed concepts and practices related to mentoring (Merriam, 1983; Daloz, 1986; Galbraith and Cohen, 1995; Cohen, 1995). Traditionally, the mentoring relationship is depicted as a rather unidirectional process in which a more experienced person provides guidance, support, and opportunities for socialization to someone who is more of a novice. Yet because mentoring is a special kind of giving that serves as a way of passing one's legacy to another person, it is potentially beneficial to both parties in the transaction.

Because of the unequal power relationship involved in most mentoring situations, it is somewhat rare for these relationships to evolve into partnerships characterized by a more or less equal give and take. Yet sometimes this can happen. Since 1980, the two of us have worked to form a special bond that we believe has transcended the boundaries of traditional mentorship into a working relationship characterized by a degree of mutuality characteristic of the notion of partnership underlying the premise of this sourcebook. In this chapter, we share our personal story of how this working relationship evolved from a traditional mentoring situation into a synergistic partnership contributing to major personal and professional growth in both of our lives.

How Our Relationship Began

In fall 1979, Ralph began his doctoral program at Syracuse University and Roger was serving as professor and chair of adult education at Iowa State University. The following fall, Roger moved to Syracuse to fill the position of chair of the adult education program. Ralph was assigned to serve as Roger's graduate assistant. Initially, this relationship was based largely on Ralph seeking help, advice, and guidance from Roger in performing his assistantship duties. However, it soon became clear that we had much in common in terms of our professional interests in self-directed learning and educational gerontology.

In the first few years, our relationship evolved naturally and incrementally out of mutual respect for each other's ability and an evolving openness and personal trust that might best be described simply as "compatibility." The relationship was accelerated for at least three reasons. The first was our shared interest in self-direction in learning and gerontology. Because of this, it was natural for Roger to chair Ralph's dissertation on the relationship between self-directed learning readiness and life satisfaction among older adults (Brockett, 1983).

Second, Ralph's initial work as a graduate assistant enabled us to work together on various projects, including Roger's editorship of *Lifelong Learning: The Adult Years*. During the following year, though Ralph was not formally assigned as a graduate assistant, Roger invited him to co-teach (as an equal partner) a graduate course on educational gerontology. In this same year, we also prepared a proposal for a federal grant; while the proposal was not funded, producing it allowed the two of us to further gain a sense of the synergy that has been so crucial to how we work.

Third, in 1982 Roger received approval to develop an innovative "Weekend Scholar" graduate option in adult education. In doing so, he was able to hire Ralph as a new nontenure-track assistant professor to recruit and help coordinate the program for a two-year period. During the two years that Ralph was on the Syracuse faculty, we began talking about more ambitious writing projects, one of which (nearly a decade later) was published as *Self-Direction in Adult Learning: Perspectives on Theory, Research, and Practice* (Brockett and Hiemstra, 1991).

In fall 1984, Ralph left Syracuse to join the faculty at Montana State University; in 1988 he moved to his current position at the University of Tennessee, Knoxville. During these years, Roger was actively engaged as principal investigator of the Syracuse University Kellogg Project, a multimillion dollar effort to bridge the use of technology and the development of historical scholarship in adult education. In May 1996, Roger left Syracuse University to pursue further work as a writer, consultant, and independent businessperson. It was in the years after we were no longer working at the same institution that the more traditional mentoring relationship began to evolve into a true partnership. Perhaps the best way to relate the journey each of us took as we moved toward our partnership is to describe the journey through the separate lenses of our individual experiences.

Roger's Story

If you are a "Peanuts" fan you know that Snoopy usually starts his perennially rejected manuscripts with "It was a dark and stormy night." Well, my and

Ralph's relationship actually began the same way. My wife and I arrived in Syracuse on a late afternoon in March 1980 for my initial set of interviews pertaining to a position. We made our way to a Holiday Inn near the campus to await my activities, which were to begin the next day. At about 3 A.M., we were awakened by a howling wind and, looking out the window, saw a horrendous snowstorm in progress. I said to Janet that I doubted many of my interview activities would take place that day.

However, when I exited the hotel at about 7:30 A.M., there was Ralph Brockett awaiting me in his automobile to escort me on my travels around campus that day and to ensure that I did indeed make all my appointments. Thus began the relationship that developed into one of mutual respect, admiration, and genuine friendship.

Before we even got to campus, Ralph mentioned that he was familiar with my publications—which I supposed was wise on his part, considering that I might become his teacher—and that he was especially interested in my work on self-directed learning and aging. Sort of incidentally, he also noted that he needed a permanent adviser and dissertation chair. I did not think much of it at the time, as I had other things on my mind, but he did not forget.

I was offered and accepted the position and, on my arrival at Syracuse University the next fall semester, Ralph was assigned as my graduate assistant and as one of my doctoral advisees. He served diligently and conscientiously as a graduate assistant and exhibited a maturity that was immediately obvious. He noted to me fairly early in the semester that he wanted to pursue a professorial career, so we fairly easily fell into a mentoring relationship. I don't think it was anything either of us really understood in terms of what could develop, but my respect for Ralph's abilities quickly turned into his assuming increasing responsibilities in departmental administration.

Within a year, I was asking Ralph to take responsibility for a few of my class sessions or to lecture on certain topics in my courses, to co-teach a graduate course with me, to carry out some research related to my responsibilities as editor of *Lifelong Learning: The Adult Years,* and to help me plan for future graduate program efforts. I also encouraged Ralph to undertake some of his own scholarly efforts, and we did some initial planning for his dissertation.

Ralph was also instrumental in the development of what became known as the "Weekend Scholar" program, an off-campus graduate program that ran for several years and met the graduate training needs of hundreds of people in several upstate New York cities. After completion of his dissertation, Ralph was hired as an assistant professor at Syracuse University and helped to coordinate and teach in one of these weekend programs. During this period, we had an opportunity to co-teach several courses, further enhancing our respect for each other's abilities.

Ralph's dissertation, as noted earlier, was on self-directed learning, and it eventually resulted in several scholarly projects for Ralph. During these writing efforts, Ralph often sought my advice and feedback. My admiration for Ralph's research, writing, and editing abilities grew continually, and while

Ralph was still in his doctoral program, we engaged in our first coauthored publication work, along with another person (Brockett, Hiemstra, and Penland, 1982).

Unfortunately, Ralph was not on a tenure track at Syracuse, so he left in the summer of 1994 for a position elsewhere. Our partnership continued, however, and although distance constrained us, we found it fairly easy to work together on writing projects, using several techniques that we will share later in this chapter. We have continued working with our mutual interest in self-direction in adult learning, but more recently we have added a shared commitment to the broad areas of ethical practice in adult education and how humanistic thought and other belief systems play a part in determining the ways adult educators make ethical decisions. Thus, more than seventeen years after our first meeting, we continue to explore old horizons in new ways while looking toward new horizons for our partnership.

Ralph's Story

I am one of those fortunate people who reflect on my graduate days with a lasting sense of joy and fondness. To be sure, it was sometimes a difficult and confusing time, filled with financial difficulty and personal adjustment. And as someone who was relatively new and inexperienced and several years younger than most of my student colleagues, in a field where professional experience is a hallmark of credibility, early on I found myself questioning whether I really belonged in doctoral study at that time. Yet, unlike most graduate students, I had a clear vision of why I was there: I wanted to be a professor of adult education, to work with students, and to engage in scholarship. This vision is what I carried with me into my very first day as a graduate student at Syracuse, and it remains to this day what I professionally hold closest to my heart.

Roger Hiemstra, more than any other person I know, embodies that spirit, and I could sense this almost from the first time I met him. On the morning after that "dark and stormy night" Roger described, I was delighted to be the person to pick Roger up. Several years earlier, I had read some of his research on older adults' learning projects, and I recall that I was quick to impress on him that this was essentially the direction I hoped to take in my own research. Needless to say, I was delighted when he accepted the position, and I was eager to work as his graduate assistant during the coming year.

What struck me almost immediately were two images of Roger: the first was of a highly disciplined, organized, and focused person who got things done in an efficient, competent manner. He was relentless in his quest to create new ideas and opportunities and to make things happen. At the same time, I saw a man who was kind, patient, and caring. I was (and continue to be) amazed at how well Roger is able to pull off both of these seemingly diametrically opposed approaches. For me, as a protégé, it meant that I had a mentor who could motivate me and get me to take action, yet give me the space to be my own person and create my own professional identity. Because pretentiousness is so far removed from Roger's basic character, I rarely felt intimidated in the presence of this man who was clearly a national leader in our field. What I felt was respect, admiration, and pride. During the two years of my doctoral program when I worked with Roger, I found myself looking forward to going to the office each day because there was always something new and interesting to explore.

Perhaps the greatest lesson I learned from Roger early on was a basic unselfishness. In 1980, Roger was invited to write a chapter on self-directed learning for an edited book. Due to some other time commitments, he offered me the opportunity to serve as second author if I would be willing to write the initial draft of the chapter. Needless to say, I was delighted! I did my part and submitted it to Roger. After we worked on a second draft, we added a third author. But when it came time to submit the final manuscript, instead of listing me as second or third author, Roger listed my name as the lead author. This one act of pure unselfishness taught me more about the kind of professor that I wish (and strive) to be than anything else I've learned or experienced since.

Over time, as Roger's and my trust and respect for each other grew, we began to talk about new ways to work together. A grant proposal, a book idea, and the "Weekend Scholar" program all became points where we could connect professionally and spend quality personal time. As Roger began to trust me with more and more of the administrative duties of the program, he also began to share with me some of the ins and outs of academic political life. He did not have to do this, but his willingness to do so was important to my future development and, I suspect, also gave him a confidant with whom he could share and brainstorm on pressing issues in the political environment of the department and college.

When I joined the faculty at Syracuse in 1982, our relationship began to take a new direction. Clearly, I still viewed Roger as my mentor and because of my trust in his judgment would usually defer to him on key issues. But, even as a graduate student, I always felt free to express my views when they differed from Roger's. This, I believe, has been essential to our developing partnership. When Roger and I write, we both are very open about suggesting changes. I never for a moment hold back in suggesting that Roger change a sentence, section, or idea in a piece of writing because he is senior to me or because he was my major professor; we just don't work that way. Likewise, Roger does not have to concern himself with "bruising the ego" of his former protégé by being critical of something I have written. I think that the key element that sustains our scholarly partnership is *trust*. Over the years, we have come to recognize that if we disagree strongly on a point, we will talk it out and make changes; otherwise, we simply defer to a natural sense of give and take, trusting that ultimately our views will come together.

How We Work

What began as a fairly typical mentoring relationship has evolved into a true partnership built on mutual respect, admiration, and trust. Although the majority of our collaborative efforts are on scholarship, we use our close friendship to talk about personal relationships or occupational trials and tribulations, and we often turn to each other when one of us simply needs a second opinion. We have been witness to growth, change, crisis, and opportunity in each other's lives and have "been there" for each other at many such times over the years. In 1983, for example, on the day after Ralph's daughter was born, Roger and his family were on hand at the hospital, offering congratulations and assistance. In 1991, when Syracuse University faced severe financial difficulties and announced the closing of several programs, including adult education, Ralph was the first person to call Roger to offer personal support. Thus, over the years, as each of us has faced major personal and professional crises and challenges, our partnership has made it possible for each of us to open ourselves to the needs of the other in a way that far transcends shared interests in scholarship.

This is not at all to say that we are carbon copies of each other (interestingly, among our professional colleagues, we sometimes find Ralph being called "Roger"—or vice versa). Besides the nearly sixteen years in age that separate us, Roger's background is rural, while Ralph's is blue-collar urban. Roger is an early riser who as a beginning assistant professor used to take pride in doing his writing in the hours before sunup; Ralph typically finds his second wind for writing in the late evening hours. Roger's avocational passions are gardening and barbershop music, while Ralph loves rock music, jazz, and hockey. But we both share a passion for good pizza, our children, backgammon, adult education, and our basic belief in the potential of people. We have never had a serious disagreement over any topic or situation, although we frequently nag each other when one of us falls behind on a writing deadline. We are proud to claim each other among our closest friends.

So, then, how does the work get done, when we have lived from six hundred to two thousand miles apart during most of the years of our partnership? Over the years, we have developed a working relationship that is maintained via phone calls and electronic mail. We frequently send initial scholarly ideas and chapter, book, or paper outlines to each other electronically. This facilitates quick revisions and finalizing of such material. Indeed, we have found that at times we are able to respond to each other more quickly via e-mail than we did when our offices were side by side at Syracuse University!

We begin most projects by asking if the other would like to be involved with some idea we have. The invitations probably run about 50–50 as to who invites whom. We don't always take each other up on it because our lives don't always run on the same schedule, or, on occasion, we simply may not have the inclination or energy to get involved in a particular project. However, more often than not, we find ourselves enticed into the project, often for the simple reason that it opens another door for us to work together.

Interestingly, we have come to realize that we often do our best work when we are face to face. We try to spend a day or two before or after at least one national conference each year on our mutual scholarly activities. Whenever possible, we have traveled to each other's homes for one or more days, especially when we need to finalize some aspect of a writing project. On one occasion, though Ralph's family was four days from making a cross-country move, we nonetheless set aside an afternoon in Montana to work on a chapter. Other times, Ralph has been able to make side trips to Syracuse to spend time at the Hiemstra household ("slumming," as Roger's daughter once laughingly put it).

This time together is especially important because our thinking and writing styles are quite similar. It is not unusual for one of us to finish the other person's thought. We usually can improve on each other's initial stabs at putting down an idea or writing a paragraph. Occasionally when one of us becomes stuck on an idea, the other can stimulate the thinking anew by trying out some new angle.

When we are actually working together, a favorite technique is for one of us to sit at the computer keyboard while the other "talks" the ideas, frequently from an outline, about the topic at hand. Synergy usually takes over at this point, and the sentences flowing out usually improve as each has his say. We often take turns doing this, so the ideas can benefit from different points of view.

For example, during the initial efforts to develop expanded chapter outlines, create some actual writing, and prepare notes on needed references, quotations, and supporting materials for a book in progress, we stayed one extra day after a conference and completed most of the writing in the manner described above. Then we went to the airport, found an electrical outlet near a restaurant, ate lunch, and finished the process, including making notes on the next steps for each of us. (Of course, some might question the sanity of people who would sacrifice a day in Florida in March to do this, but that's a part of the price we accept for our partnership.)

Some Closing Reflections

In this discussion, our intent was to provide an inside look at how the two of us have been able to forge a partnership that we believe has been mutually beneficial for many years. It is important to remember that there is no single correct way to form a partnership. In writing this chapter, we realize that some readers may think we are simply coming across as a couple of "buddies" who are "swapping war stories" in an uncritical way. But to see only this aspect is to miss the real point of the story. The real significance is that sometimes partnerships can be found when one leaves oneself open to possibility. We do not advocate our partnership as a model and, indeed, while we have both had mentoring relationships over the years in which we take great pride and we have both had successful coauthoring experiences with other colleagues in our field, this partnership is unlike any other that either of us has experienced, and it has grown and thrived for over seventeen years and hundreds (and thousands) of miles.

While we do not propose ours as *the* model for a successful partnership, we offer the following general observations that might be useful considerations for those who are seeking, considering, or are in the process of forming a partnership:

- It is important to recognize that there is no single correct route toward forming a partnership. Sometimes it is the result of a common vision. At other times, it comes from a mutual desire to interact with another like-minded person.
- While some partnerships have an ebb and flow, so that the partnership dissolves once the task at hand has been completed, other partnerships can transcend this task orientation; hence, partners may find themselves using their synergy to explore problems and topics that go far beyond the boundaries of what brought them together.
- The successful shift from a mentoring relationship to a partnership requires a certain character on the part of both participants. For the mentor, it means a willingness to unselfishly "let go" in order for the protégé to develop his or her identity apart from that of the mentor. It can sometimes mean watching while the protégé surpasses the professional accomplishments of the mentor in some areas of endeavor. For the protégé, it means being willing to reduce one's psychic dependence on the mentor. For both, it means a sense of loyalty and trust that are reflected in a long-term commitment to the relationship.
- There is true synergy in a good partnership, and the writing products, new ideas, and new ways of thinking that result will usually be much more powerful and productive than would be possible through an individual effort.
- It is important to understand that one probably can never truly directly repay one's mentor. The way to do this is by working to become an effective mentor for one's own protégés.

Conclusion

Our experiences in developing a mentoring relationship that eventually evolved into a partnership have been very positive. However, we recognize that there are potential pitfalls:

- Living a distance apart can slow the rate of accomplishment, although electronic communication increasingly mitigates this concern.
- Care must be taken in establishing the mentoring relationship or partnership so that one person does not become too dependent on the other. Certainly both partners need to be sensitive to issues of diversity when they differ in gender, race, cultural background, or other such factors.
- It is important that decisions regarding such issues as order of authorship, division of workload, and deadlines for completion be established early.

In conclusion, we believe that while the transition from a mentoring relationship to a synergistic partnership is often difficult to achieve, we have found the rewards to far outweigh the risks and costs. While we recognize that our situation is neither practical nor feasible in many situations, we believe that our story offers some insights into how it might be possible for others to build such relationships.

References

Brockett, R. G. "Self-Directed Learning Readiness and Life Satisfaction Among Older Adults." Doctoral dissertation, Syracuse University, 1982. Dissertation Abstracts International, vol. 44, p. 42A.

Brockett, R. G., and Hiemstra, R. *Self-Direction in Adult Learning: Perspectives on Theory, Research, and Practice.* New York: Routledge, 1991.

Brockett, R. G., Hiemstra, R., and Penland, P. R. "Self-Directed Learning." In C. Klevins (ed.), *Materials and Methods in Adult and Continuing Education.* Canoga Park, Calif.: Klevens Publications, 1982.

Cohen, N. H. *Mentoring Adult Learners: A Guide for Educators and Trainers.* Malabar, Fla.: Krieger, 1995.

Daloz, L. A. *Effective Teaching and Mentoring: Realizing the Transformational Power of Adult Learning Experiences.* San Francisco: Jossey-Bass, 1986.

Galbraith, M. W., and Cohen, N. H. (eds.). *Mentoring: New Strategies and Challenges.* New Directions for Adult and Continuing Education, no. 66. San Francisco: Jossey-Bass, 1995.

Merriam, S. B. "Mentors and Protégés: A Critical Review of the Literature." *Adult Education Quarterly,* 1983, 33 (3), 161–173.

ROGER HIEMSTRA is a writer, consultant, and independent businessperson who lives in Fayetteville, New York. For over twenty-five years, he served as professor of adult education at the University of Nebraska–Lincoln, Iowa State University, and Syracuse University.

RALPH G. BROCKETT is professor of adult education at the University of Tennessee, Knoxville, and former editor-in-chief of New Directions for Adult and Continuing Education.

Cohort partnerships offer an effective way to help learners succeed in long-term learning efforts, such as completing a dissertation.

Cohort Partnerships: A Pragmatic Approach to Doctoral Research

James E. Witte, Waynne B. James

We believe that the power of collaborative partnerships can play an important role helping students move successfully through the dissertation process. In this chapter, we will describe our experience with a cohort research group at the University of South Florida (USF). This cohort group helped several students complete their doctoral programs while contributing to a collective body of research that extends beyond the parameters of any single study.

The Dilemma of Doctoral Study

On initial examination, the process of completing advanced graduate work in pursuit of the doctorate appears fairly simple: take some courses, then write a dissertation. Further examination quickly erodes the simplicity. Following acceptance into a program, one would normally begin a program of studies reflecting both the desires of the individual and the institution. Such programs often involve taking courses in sequence. Students find that some courses are more demanding than others. The balancing of specific courses of study may be accomplished by conferring with the major professor, a trusted faculty member, or fellow students.

Once a specific course is selected, the student's activities are driven by a variety of predictable requirements and expectations. The schedule of classes tells them where to be and what time to be there. The syllabus governs the course requirements. For instance, the course requirements may include three papers, a presentation, a midterm and final examination, or other specific course requirements. So begins the coursework, and so it continues until all

NEW DIRECTIONS FOR ADULT AND CONTINUING EDUCATION, no. 79, Fall 1998 © Jossey-Bass Publishers

necessary courses have been completed. Course after course, semester after semester, a process unfolds that is reasonably stable and predictable.

Then a strange thing happens: the coursework is complete and the examinations are over—sort of. The advanced graduate student is now in candidacy. This phase of doctoral study lacks the predictable security brought about by the schedule and syllabus. Here, for most people, the question arises: What next? Again, the apparently simple question brings an apparently simple answer: prepare a proposal, and defend it; prepare a final dissertation, and defend it. Along the way, most students seek help from the major professor, committee members, trusted faculty members, and fellow students.

Interaction with fellow students is described by Youngs in the *American Educational Research Association Graduate Student Newsletter.* Youngs (1997–1998) reports, in part: "I found it helpful to get to know some veteran graduate students in Division K at this university. I received guidance and support from these individuals as I went through the process of preparing a research proposal, watched as they rehearsed conference presentations and job interviews, and listened to them describe their efforts to balance graduate work with familial, social, and political commitments. In addition, some of them have helped me negotiate relationships with faculty members and understand and accept that my relationships with certain faculty will be limited and/or unsatisfying" (p. 5).

If students naturally gravitate to one another, and we believe they do, it appears that the formation of groups, either formal or informal, is a natural by-product of the educational process. Rather than relying on the informal group, a slightly more formalized group results when cohorts are formed. These cohorts may evolve from common coursework experiences, study groups, or related interests in research topics.

The University of South Florida Research Cohort

Drawing from experiences at a previous university, the major professor recognized that the concept of a dissertation cohort group provided a viable means to simultaneously manage a substantial number of doctoral students. Maintaining that Robert J. Havighurst's social roles research from the 1950s was outdated and inappropriate in today's society, she actively encouraged students to pursue a cohort group research project.

Approximately eight years ago, six doctoral students in an adult development course organized themselves into a cohort group to explore Havighurst's (1957) concept of social roles, which had become outdated and inappropriate in today's society. From biweekly meetings after class to weekly meetings devoted totally to social roles, the group researched, conceptualized, discussed, and supported each other for several years.

Faculty reception to the overall concept of the research project was mixed. On one hand, there was the perception that collaborative efforts were lower in status than individual efforts. On the other hand, collegiality and teamwork were openly espoused. There seemed to be a sense that a collaborative project was too long, too big, or too complex to handle.

When we initially used the term *group dissertation,* many faculty members were horrified, thinking there would be one project (dissertation) written by five or six individuals. When we assured faculty that each individual would write his or her own dissertation, the skepticism abated. Eventually we replaced the term *group dissertation* with the term *lines of inquiry.* As more faculty members served on the dissertation committees or on various instrument validation panels, excitement about the actual project and the process grew.

Our advocates came from a variety of departments. Probably most fortuitous was the support from the Research and Measurement Department. Fortunately, we were able to intrigue a measurement expert, a research design specialist, and a statistician with the process. Their input and expertise were crucial to ensuring that the project would withstand the rigor and scrutiny of the research community. Other departments and individuals proved especially beneficial, notably a technical writer, faculty members from the Gerontology Department, and individuals from the Educational Leadership Department.

Students were attracted to the cohort group for a variety of reasons. Some were attracted because of the subject. The research itself was based on updating and validating the 1950s social roles research of Havighurst. Students tended to match their particular interests to specific social roles. For instance, one student had a particularly strong background in physical health and fitness; therefore, exploring the Havighurst role of leisure time consumer was a logical choice. Occasionally a student would attempt to join the cohort group, motivated by the false assumption that cohort research produced an easy dissertation. These few students quickly learned that *cohort-supported research* is not a euphemism for *easy.* The rigorous methods and standards within the group as moderated by the major professor either produced a functioning team member or the student voluntarily withdrew to seek other alternatives.

Initially our meetings began as biweekly meetings following evening classes. These progressed to sessions after class, and once most of the students had completed their coursework, we met once a week on an evening when most had no regular commitments. Initial meetings were informal; however, as everyone progressed, we felt the need to structure our sessions in a more formal manner. Consequently formal agendas and minutes were instituted, with the major professor assuming primary responsibility for ensuring that these items were made available in a timely manner. As demands on group members escalated, less prominence was given to the agendas and minutes. Although all group members agreed on the importance of these items, no individual assumed responsibility for creating agendas, and subsequently the process lapsed. In hindsight, the maintenance of agendas and minutes would have proved beneficial by reducing frustration and competition for attention.

There were several positive attributes of this cohort group. Cohort groups in general provide an extension of the systematic education experience. Although our group was not as regimented as the classroom experience (lacked such items as schedules and syllabi), it was structured with regular meetings and indicators of individual and group progress, thereby providing a modified continuation of previous educational experience. The cohort also provided a framework for mutual learning. Mutual learning is encouraged throughout the education process and particularly emphasized at the advanced graduate level. As the students gained experience and expertise, the role of the major professor was transformed from "sage on stage" to "guide on the side." Typically a single faculty member can mentor and guide a group of students, reducing time, effort, and redundancy when compared with mentoring each student individually. This economy of effort benefits the student. Within the recent cohort group at the University of South Florida, five out of six members finalized their dissertations within a single semester (after a year or more of research); the sixth finished the following semester. It is highly unlikely that all these students would have experienced timely completion without the benefit of the cohort group.

Dynamics of the Cohort Process

Because we found no education models for dissertation cohort research groups, we developed a process model. Our reflections on the process include observations on the structure, roles, change, and personalities, as well as cohesive and disruptive forces of the group.

Routine meetings and use of an agenda were part of establishing predictable structure and reasonable expectations. Throughout this experience, we found that our cohort research was more apt to be productive when we met at regularly scheduled times, set specific (but flexible) agendas, and established appropriate time lines. By establishing a reasonable time line, each group member's possibility of project completion was enhanced. Throughout the time line, various critical points were identified: completion of introduction, literature review and methods chapters; field testing; data gathering; and statistical analysis. When the individual time lines were arrayed, patterns of critical points and activities emerged. Some critical points required extensive group support, others required less group support.

As relationships within the group began to solidify and roles were defined, we established a process that encouraged members to be mutually supportive, to share resources, and to create partnerships. A mutual dependency developed in which group members relied on one another to read drafts and gather data, as well as offer time and expertise. Supporting others often conflicted with the individual's own research efforts. A climate of trust was essential and needed to be established early in the cohort process. In essence, group members had to know with reasonable certainty that "if I help you now, you will help me later." Without establishing trust based on actions, the group could have degenerated to a collection of "me first" individuals, and the benefits of the cohort concept would have been lost.

One positive outcome of the cohort process was shared resources. Generally, the research group members purchased stationery and miscellaneous supplies as needed. Students shared the costs of acquiring and duplicating relevant dissertations and other materials. If one person found something useful for everyone, he or she made copies for each of us. If the information was appropriate only for a specific area of research, that information was routinely passed on to the person who needed it. When a group of us went to the University of Chicago to examine Robert Havighurst's papers, information on specific topics was gathered and shared with the appropriate individuals.

Relationships within the group changed over time. Different needs or activities promoted different working relationships. Cohort partnerships, built on trust and commitment, flourish long after the academic projects have been completed.

Not all students progressed along the time line at an equal rate. Some seemed to have more available time, perhaps more expertise or a higher degree of comfort with the process; for whatever reason, some students began to move at a faster pace than others. This natural phenomenon was not necessarily a deterrent to the group. Those who progressed rapidly or neared completion were affectionately designated as "lead dog," as in Alaskan dogsled teams. All dogs pull the sled, but they do so in a sequenced, orderly fashion. As the "lead dogs" progressed and completed their respective dissertations, they were replaced by other group members. New members seeking a similar academic path were then brought into the group, and the process continued.

We very quickly learned the relevance of personality to the group process. The cohort group became a microcosm in which personalities strongly influenced individual member roles within the group. Group members assumed a variety of roles at different times. Examples include bringing humor to the group, observing passively, blocking or attempting to dominate the process, or a variety of other roles. Sometimes these roles worked to the group's advantage, sometimes not. In retrospect, we would urge those considering doctoral research cohort groups to openly discuss and develop applied skills in dealing with the group process and group member roles. Not only do we feel that an increased awareness of group processes would reduce potential friction, but in doing so, the group would gain efficiency and actually reduce research time and improve the final products.

Fortunately our cohort group possessed many of the cohesive forces needed to develop an effectively functioning group. Since the entire group centered on a common research topic, shared goals and methods were evident. However, other factors such as the expression of individual differences, sensitivity to individual needs, a range of individual contributions, and encouragement were also evident. Two of the most important forces were shared decision making and norms of behavior (both verbalized and understood). One example of a group-developed norm was that each group member was allowed one night to irrationally vent frustration during the group meeting. Venting of frustration, by design, seemed to strengthen group member bonds, tolerance, and understanding of common experiences.

Disruptive forces also played a part in the dynamics of the cohort group process. Such factors as interpersonal conflicts, morale, dichotomy between leadership and power, and differences in perspective sometimes affected the group in a less than positive manner. Some group members were comfortable with and sought more highly structured activities, while others, including the major professor, neither desired nor sought a rigid structure. Group members sometimes viewed one another as either too prescriptive or too disorganized, which led to frustration. The polar positions were greatly diminished when we recognized the dilemma and actively sought mutually agreeable solutions. Another disruptive force was the relationship between leadership and power. Since the major professor was perceived as having considerable power and influence over the process and ultimately whether students graduated, conflict or confrontation was a serious matter. Conflict sometimes arose when the major professor made decisions that considered the entire project and quality research methods and design standards, but group members perceived these decisions as dictatorial or arbitrary. When the basis for dictum was understood and accepted by the group, resistance to dictum was greatly reduced. This disruptive force was a product of the dual form of collaboration discussed in the following paragraphs.

Hafernik, Messerschmitt, and Vandrick (1997) espouse that collaboration occurs in various dimensions. Two of the broad categories of collaboration, according to Hafernik and colleagues, are hierarchical and equal. They explain that "Hierarchical relationships may basically be mentorships such as those of a major professor and graduate students. . . . Truly equal relationships seem less common than hierarchical ones" (p. 32).

Our cohort group incorporated both dimensions of collaboration: hierarchical and equal. The faculty-student relationship by tradition is hierarchical in nature. The relationships between the students, on the other hand, are generally based on equality. The amalgamation of both dimensions formed a unique model for collaborative arrangements.

The hierarchical nature of the USF collaborative effort was evidenced by the dominant role often assumed by the major professor. This dominant role reflected university expectations and responsibilities. She served as the gatekeeper for university procedures and graduate school requirements, as well as overall research study rigor. In addition, in case of dispute, she was the final arbiter.

The students also had a major role in formulating procedures, making decisions, or developing new ideas. At times, the major professor was a team member of equal standing with other team members. For example, when scoring interviews, team members independently provided an overall score for each interview. The major professor provided one of these scores, and her score was substantiated and defended with vigor equal to that of any other group member.

Benefits and Limitations of the Cohort Process

We would love to be able to say that everyone got along perfectly with everyone else in the group, and that everything was completed thoroughly, smoothly, correctly, and on time. However, no such fairy tale occurred: some things worked, some things didn't. Based on our experience, we perceive five potential benefits of cohort group research: framework, support system, contribution to field, multiple perspectives, and skill enhancement.

One of the major benefits of the cohort group was that it provided a framework and a process for increasing productivity. This framework aided in breaking down the psychological and logistical barriers that often hamper academic research. We found that a research framework was particularly important for the neophyte researcher. Without a framework to guide the researcher through the process, unnecessary effort and resources were expended. For example, one non-cohort student is currently working on his third dissertation proposal. A clear framework identifying sequence, milestones, events, and reasonable expectations allowed ordered, disciplined research to occur.

The cohort research group also functioned as a support group that provided camaraderie and a sense of belonging among the members. As individual members progressed, each group member offered encouragement and provided added incentives to continue producing. A spirit based on a philosophy described as "if they can do it, I can do it!" frequently served as motivation. Friendly competition, in the sense of "I want to keep up with the group," often provided a strong but unanticipated motivation to finish.

By appropriately sharing the load (for example, data gathering, draft review, discussion), an extremely complex research project was undertaken with assurance that many facets of the project could be addressed. In that sense, a contribution to the field of adult education was accomplished using fewer resources than if one individual had attempted the project alone. One person would be incapable of studying all of Havighurst's social roles without writing the "Great American Dissertation" or taking an estimated twenty years to complete the research. Individual research purposefully conducted within the parameters of a larger project can culminate in a far greater contribution to the field than individual efforts alone.

The fourth valuable asset of the cohort group was the varied perspectives individual members brought to the group. These multiple perspectives allowed for more critical analysis and reflection than one would customarily find between only the student and the mentor. These differing perspectives and experiences proved crucial at several major points. For example, one aspect of the Havighurst research, the spouse/partner interview, underwent major revision because one of the group members as a test case did not fall into the expected role pattern. The individual research was strengthened as a result of group involvement. On another issue, gender differences were potentially affecting interview scoring results, so it was necessary to install safeguards to compensate for gender biases that might occur. Again, the additional steps and safeguards developed by the group contributed to a more rigorous performance model.

Finally, the successful cohort group provided a performance model that embraced many of the skills required of the researcher: the ability to conceptualize, to communicate both in written and oral form, and to develop a sense of trustworthiness and confidence. To withstand the scrutiny of peers, the individual group member had to consistently prepare and hone the requisite academic skills. There is a recognized emphasis on teamwork as a venue for success both within and outside the academic world. The cohort group process helps develop team skills and attitudes and creates a learning environment that best puts into practice the concepts and constructs promoted within the college or university system.

While there are benefits to cohort research, there are also limitations. We can identify five major problem areas associated with cohort groups: management, conflict and competition, dependency, narrow focus, and individual constraints.

An improperly managed cohort group can become a source of conflict for both peers and the major professor. Students may compete for time with the major professor or for group time to focus on a particular item of interest. If a student is shunted to one side, delayed until the next meeting, or otherwise thwarted, the student is left with unfulfilled expectations or needs. In that situation, the potential for conflict heightens. Time and activities must be carefully managed in order to meet both needs and expectations of all group members, including the major professor.

One of the problems we experienced in our cohort group was the influence of personalities, which affected all phases of the research process. Along with various strengths, each member brought to the group his or her unique and sometimes idiosyncratic personality. Personality-driven behaviors sometimes caused tension during group meetings. Particularly dominant personalities would attempt to monopolize time, manipulate the agenda, and exhibit demands that inhibited the group process. Group functions returned to normal when these behaviors were channeled into positive actions and the needs of each member were considered and met.

Frequently, students joining the cohort initially seemed to form dependency relationships. One common sign of dependency was to let the major professor review and approve each change, review each draft, or have input into each new thought. This dependency was counterproductive to the student's intellectual growth and further disrupted the group process by demanding inordinate amounts of the major professor's time. When the group managed themselves, with the oversight of the major professor, group functions went more smoothly.

A fourth problem was the tendency to strictly replicate the procedures of previously successful cohort members. This narrow focus was intellectually stifling. The work of previous members provided general procedural guidelines; however, students had to strive to maintain ownership of their work. The cohort group neither abrogates nor replaces individual responsibility.

The fifth problem dealt with individual constraints. Graduate students easily find multiple sources of distraction: finances, time, job, family, academic demands and expectations, to name a few. The typical doctoral student balances the demands of home, employment, and school requirements. Students may find that the magnitude and frequency of project demands result in heightened conflict. Cohorts can add an additional burden when the student must adjust individual goal pursuit in order to aid or assist other group members. For instance, if one of the group members was gathering data, the remaining group members would support the task. This was sometimes seen as an additional burden that detracted from individual effort.

Strategies for Cohort Success

The challenge in successfully implementing the concept of a dissertation cohort research group is to accentuate the benefits of the process while minimizing the negative issues. To replicate the benefits we found in our cohort research, we believe it is necessary to be committed to the cohort process, which is structured to account for acceptance of change, recognition of individual personality differences, and management of both the cohesive and disruptive forces affecting the process.

Cohort group success is largely dependent on the commitment of the major professor/adviser and the individual group members. Commitment, trust, and respect are absolutely essential for cohort success. The training necessary to develop sufficient skill and understanding to contribute to the work of a colleague requires extra effort and a higher degree of commitment and trust than is normally found in independent research. Additional commitment is needed to acquire the skills and understanding and the trust that a colleague will return support in a like manner. This is an integral part of the cohort process. When commitment and trust are lacking, the group effort dwindles to activities perceived as self-serving and noncooperative, with one person slowing down the process of the others.

A mutually agreed-upon structure, time lines, and process understanding will potentially reduce group friction. Group members may also agree on sanctions or penalties for noncompliance, lack of commitment, or creation of new demands that have not been previously accepted. An agenda for each cohort meeting is an essential tool for management of time, activities, and, to some extent, individuals. For instance, when the group agrees to meet at a specified time and place, all members need to make an attempt to attend consistently. The same night of the week in the same room becomes an extension of the class schedule, a previously acquired and accepted behavioral pattern. Although some of our colleagues may claim this is not the characteristic we want to engender in our students, we found that it became a very practical consideration for doctoral students who also had work, family, and community responsibilities.

The agenda corresponds to the course syllabus. By establishing an agenda for weekly meetings, group members have reasonable predictability concerning what is expected of them and, in turn, what they can expect from others. The structural nature of the agenda reduces the incidence of individual students vying for sole attention or monopolizing the group's time. The agenda can also serve as a minor sanction for those group members who fail to perform. A common activity may be for cohort group members to review and provide feedback and suggestions on the written work of other group members. Should the student fail to prepare the materials for review during the time allotted, that time may be divided among the students who are prepared and future time allotted to the student who failed to perform. Students may initially propose changes to the agenda when they are unprepared. For instance, rather than review draft documents, a student might propose to discuss data treatment methods. This change, although it appears minor, violates the expectations of the group. By adjusting the agenda to place the change at the end of the meeting's activities, the group recognizes that students who are prepared will have their needs met, yet demonstrates sufficient flexibility to accommodate the needs of others.

As students matured in research skills and abilities, their roles in the group would often change from interested recipient to proactive participant. As the process progressed, individual members out of necessity would adjust to shifts in relationships among other group members and the major professor. At the same time, the major professor adjusted to and accepted the growth of the students.

Recognizing and accepting individual differences and idiosyncrasies are essential to the cohort process. We found that we had to trust and respect one another, leave our egos outside the meeting, provide and receive constructive criticism without being overly defensive, tolerate ambiguity, deal with topics not of immediate concern, and not worry about who was working the hardest. We further believe that knowledge of and attention to group member roles and dynamics might have improved the functioning of the group.

In closing, cohort dissertation research groups reflect the power and potential of collaborative partnerships. Cohort research involves investment of time and energy and an opportunity to deal with a wide range of issues. It also allows a faculty member to work effectively with a large number of students and for the cohort group to make a contribution to a body of knowledge that would not be possible through individual efforts. We believe the benefits of cohort research groups far outweigh the limitations.

References

Hafernik, J. J., Messerschmitt, D. S., and Vandrick, S. "Collaborative Research: Why and How?" *Educational Research, 1997, 9* (12), 31–36.

Havighurst, R. J. "The Social Competence of Middle-Aged People." *Genetic Psychology Monographs, 1957, 56,* 297–375.

Youngs, P. A. "The Role of Mentoring in Graduate Education." *American Educational Research Association Graduate Student Newsletter,* Fall/Winter 1997–1998, p. 5.

JAMES E. WITTE is adjunct professor of adult and vocational education at the University of South Florida.

WAYNNE B. JAMES is professor of adult and vocational education at the University of South Florida (USF). She is adviser to the USF Social Roles Research Cohort Group.

*In this chapter, women professors of adult education reflect on their
experience of collaboration in research and writing. They discuss the
benefits and difficulties of collaboration, the various ways they go
about it, and what they learn from the experience.*

Women's Experience of
Academic Collaboration

M. Carolyn Clark, Denise B. Watson

Partnering for learning in adulthood takes different forms, depending on the
context in which the learners are situated. For those of us in higher education,
the most common form is academic collaboration. This typically means that
two or more colleagues jointly design and conduct a research project and
together write up their findings. Interestingly, while there appears to be an
increase in academic collaboration in higher education, it is a phenomenon
that itself has not been extensively researched (Baldwin and Austin, 1995).

What is it like to work collaboratively in the academy? In Chapter Five of
this book, Hiemstra and Brockett explore one aspect of such collaboration, the
unfolding dynamic of the mentor-protégé relationship. In this chapter we
would like to focus on a different aspect, the experience of women academics
in the collaborative process. There's good reason to believe that women faculty
members experience collaboration differently from men. Certainly the literature on women's psychosocial development (see, for example, Gilligan, 1982;
Josselson, 1987; and Caffarella, 1992), in arguing for the ongoing centrality of
relationship to women, would suggest that women would come to this professional relationship differently than men do. And while the limited empiri-
cal study of academic collaboration has not specifically explored the role of
gender in this process, we do know something about how women academics
think about their research. Aisenberg and Harrington (1988), in their study of

Note: We wish to thank the participants in this study who so generously shared their experiences of collaboration with us: Rosemary Caffarella, Sharan Merriam, Jovita Ross-Gordon,
Elisabeth Hayes, Daniele Flannery, Victoria Marsick, Karen Watkins, Kathy Loughlin, Eliz-
abeth Kasl, Gwendolyn Kaltoft, and Annie Brooks.

tenure-track and nontenure-track women faculty, found that women academics relate to their research in a very personal, even passionate way, in contrast to the more instrumental relationship characteristic of male academics. To begin to understand the role gender plays in academic collaboration, we need first to determine what the collaborative experience of women academics is like. That is the focus of this chapter.

The logical place to begin, we thought, is with some of the women themselves, so we initiated a conversation with a number of women academics in adult education who have extensive experience doing collaborative research. All have collaborated with various partners, both with other women and with men, but there is significant variation in their experiences. Two of the women have a long-term collaborative relationship, having written together for more than ten years. Two others are in the early stages of an extensive research project together. And four of the women are exploring the boundaries of collaboration itself by experimenting with new forms of epistemology; they describe themselves as "a group of practitioner-scholars who write and learn together, working to create a collaborative model for scholarship within the academy" (Group for Collaborative Inquiry and thINQ, 1994).

We asked these women to share with us what their experience of collaboration is like. These conversations were entirely open-ended and were conducted with small groups of the women. The sessions were audiotaped and transcribed, and each participant later reviewed and corrected their transcriptions.

In this chapter we have woven together strands from these interviews to create a larger conversation. To expand it still further, we have incorporated within it the voices of other women who have worked collaboratively and reflected on their experience of doing research together (Belenky, Clinchy, Goldberger, and Tarule, 1986; Baker and Kline, 1996; Lunsford and Ede, 1988; Kennedy, 1995). Where appropriate, we also include insights of others who have studied the process of academic collaboration itself (Ashton-Jones and Thomas, 1990; Ede and Lunsford, 1990). What follows is a kind of meta-conversation among these various women academics. We've organized the conversation thematically, following the threads generated by the women we interviewed. Our voice is in italics; the interviewees' voices are in the type like this, with the symbol § indicating the entry of a new voice into the flow. Commentary will be given apart from the conversation itself, as indicated by resumption of this typeface. We begin with the women describing what they get out of the collaborative process.

Benefits of Collaboration

All of you have lots of experience collaborating on research projects with colleagues and students. Why do you do it? What's in it for you?

§   One of the things, I think, that keeps us doing this, at least from my point of view, is that the development of the ideas is so much richer, and so much more fun. Feeling that you're isolated, trying to do this thing on your own is really tough. It's both the enrichment of the ideas, which I think would never reach the stage where they're at [if we were working alone]. . . . It's not only that, it's a good relationship. I mean, we've become very good friends.

§   [For me] collaboration [is] the time for thinking things I never think [about] in the same way otherwise and having someone else firing in ideas, so it's very much of a learning experience for me. And it's very much of a professional development experience, as well as a personal connectedness experience.

§   And the emotional kind of support dimension is really important, [too], to keep you motivated. I know that something I often experience by myself is, I end up going, "Who cares about this?" you know, "Why continue?" And being able to share the enthusiasm for what we're doing with somebody else really is important.

§   Well, it is interesting, but I'm going to have to say that it's wonderful. I mean, I wouldn't trade the collaborating [I'm doing right now] for doing this on my own in a million years, because of the discussions we get into about the data and the interpretation and the ways of thinking about it. We each have been doing reading in slightly different areas. And we bring it in and enrich the whole thing, and it's so captivating, because of the angles and the multilayered sorts of things that [come out]. . . . Just my looking at the data, I would never, in a million years, never have seen that.

§   One of the things that I feel when I do it is that my thinking gets advanced with the other person, so that there's a synergy that happens.

§   Absolutely! You know, when we each come in with sort of a sketch of some finding or something, and we plunk it up on paper, and then we talk about it and we move things around, and then the next time one of us might come back with a rearrangement of something—"Oh yeah, why didn't we see that to begin with?" It's wonderful!

§   What's, in the end, been most important to me has been the entry of everybody else's ideas into my ideas, and the chance to develop my ideas verbally with a bunch of people.

The excitement of collaboration and the synergy it creates was a common theme that ran through our interviews and was echoed in the literature. Hiemstra and Brockett (1994) and Ashton-Jones (1992) note how the combination of minds creates something greater than the sum of individual efforts. Perhaps our favorite example of this was the Ashton-Jones and Thomas (1990) interview with Mary Belenky in which Belenky described the centrality of the collaborative process to the production of *Women's Ways of Knowing*: "This book could not have been written by any single one of us, without this broader conversation. It has a scope that reflects a wide range of experiences in a wide range of institutions, and a single person couldn't have created that. I don't think a single person can get the kind of clarity that comes through working together to pull away the chaff and let the bold ideas come forth" (pp. 280–281).

All of the women we interviewed would agree that a good collaboration is an exhilarating experience. We should add, though, that no one claimed that all their experiences were of this sort. Several distinguished between types of collaboration, for example, noting that some are more instrumental—dividing up the labor on a project—than creative. And others noted the difference between collaborating with a peer and collaborating with a less experienced researcher. So comments about the value of academic collaboration need to be understood within the context of the particular type of relationship that is involved.

Process of Collaboration

So, how do you do this, exactly? How do you collaborate with someone on a research and writing project?

§   [For us it has evolved.] The first couple of things we wrote, we more or less divided them up and I wrote a piece and [she] wrote a piece and, because our styles were sufficiently compatible, we just interwove them. [Later, when we wrote a book together,] we created the idea for the book by creating a template, in terms of the theory [we had developed]. And we jointly wrote the first chapter and last chapter.

§   I think the most dramatic thing that we love to talk about is the way in which we ended up doing [our next] book, which was, I think, a real turning point for us. We began that book as we had that other one, with each of us taking half the chapters and doing a first cut. And we got all this really critical feedback.

   [Then we arranged to spend a week together to do revisions.]. . .We took our two PowerBooks, set them up side by side on the counter, and we decided that we couldn't continue to try to solve the problems in our own chapter, but instead that what we needed to do was to take each other's chapter and completely rewrite it. Then give it back to the first author to now wordsmith it after it had had this major, major rewrite. And that just turned out to work incredibly well. And we did that yet a third time [several months later] because we had revisions again after that. That really became what I would call the real first draft.

Mary Belenky outlines a similarly intimate process when she describes how she and her colleagues worked together (Ashton-Jones and Thomas, 1990). They met for three to four days of sustained conversation about their study every five weeks over a period of three years. These "pajama-party meet-ings" enabled them to bring their thinking together on the project. Their writing began with a month-long session together in which they planned out the book and decided who would write which parts. Then they circulated their drafts among one another for critique and revisions. Interestingly, they chose to circulate hard copies rather than computer disks so that their voices would remain distinct: "Because of the way my colleagues each wrote in the margin, I always knew their handwriting, and so as I worked on redrafting I had their different voices to work with" (p. 280). Belenky spoke of the writing process as "really very sensuous," as their words mingled together to form the final text.

Several of the women we interviewed spoke of a kind of mingling of ideas as part of their process of working together:

§   When we're facing a task, things immediately come to my mind, sort of like all kinds of little brain pieces firing ideas. But we have developed a certain sort of rhythm together now, so that the minute they do, [my partner] writes them down, because once I've said them, I don't remember them. It's really brainstorming. And it's just automatic: I [generate ideas], she writes [them down], then we look at [them] and take [it] from [there]. It's nothing we planned but . . .

§   But it's good because I can ask questions sometimes about the idea, so they can be developed in that way.

§   [We do something similar.] I do my thinking out loud and [my partner] does it inside. So that difference has been wonderful because I can chatter away, and she'll go sit at the computer, and out will come this thing that is both what I said and now something wholly different because she's integrated her thinking the way that she does. And so we'll take that and talk out loud again. So we'll kind of go back and forth in terms of our styles, as well.

We noted earlier that these women each had experienced various types of collaborative relationships. In discussing how they work, however, they chose to focus on those relationships where there was less of an instrumental division of tasks and more of a blending of thought and knowledge construction. Our own experience in writing this chapter together is an example of a different type of relationship—that of mentor and protégé—and how we worked together reflected that relationship. For us there was more of a division of tasks, with Carolyn taking the lead in conceptualizing and writing, and Denise assuming primary responsibility for reviewing the literature. Yet we also worked together in identifying the threads across the interviews and in selecting the elements to weave together into the larger conversation. And it was through our ongoing conversation about all this material that we worked at making sense of it together. Overall, our sense is that how all thirteen of us go about doing collaborative work reflects the nature of the particular relationship involved at that point; as the relationship develops, the style of working together also evolves.

Difficulties of Collaboration

Your descriptions so far have been very positive. What is the downside here? What kinds of problems do you face when you try to collaborate with someone?

§   I would urge caution here. . . . Collaboration can also be overwhelming. It's [definitely] more work.

§   I also think there are some fundamental values that go with collaborative writing. Things like you're willing to give up some of your ideas. . . . You have to negotiate.

§   Yeah, and [be] willing to critique and be critiqued. And not take it personally.

§   There are also issues of power involved. I think there are some basic fundamental values [involved]. If you can't give up any of that power, or you always have to be in the limelight . . . I'm not sure collaboration is really healthy or works for you.

§   What I'm always surprised about is how two people [can write] and it can come out like one person's writing. At the same time, that doesn't always happen.

§   And it's sometimes a lot of work to make it happen. Sometimes somebody's going to have to do more blending or patching or something to make the cross between the two sets of writing seem more transparent.

§   That's where one of you has to take the lead, because I don't know how you can have it come out otherwise. One person has to go through it. I've had two experiences like that where one of my coauthors was not a very good writer to begin with, the other one just had a totally different style, and it was difficult. I've gotten more cautious about who I collaborate with, for that reason, because you'll make more work for yourself.

In addition to these larger difficulties, there are the logistical problems created by geographical separation of collaborating partners, and the solutions can be costly in terms of both time and money (Hiemstra and Brockett, 1994). The women we interviewed did not downplay these issues, and they were expressed most forcefully by those in long-term collaborative relationships:

§   To get down to some kind of brass tacks, though, it's been really hard to be a group together and, speaking for myself, there's many times that I've felt, "Jesus, do I want to stay in this?" It's time-consuming, it's emotionally [costly], it's expensive because we all live in different parts of the United States—it's enormously expensive. The amount that we produce seems small compared to the amount of work that we put into producing it.

These women are remarkably direct about the difficulties involved in doing collaborative work; they certainly come to the process without illusions.

Kennedy (1995), in her reflections on three different experiences of collaboration in her career as an anthropologist, discusses the negative side of the process in some detail, describing with particular poignancy the strain on relationships that collaboration can create. What is perhaps most striking, though, in our interviews and in the literature, is the willingness of women academics to deal with these negative elements and to pay the price exacted by this process. This is a particularly strong indicator of the high value they place on collaboration.

Learning from Collaboration

One thing that struck us is how much learning goes on when you collaborate with someone.

§   Absolutely! I think we've used our writing as opportunities to get our thinking together, in a way. We used it as an opportunity to put down what we know and talk about it so that we could put the theory together.

§   And for us it's almost like co-discovery. And it's fun, because there's something quite fun about learning it at the same time. So you spark each other, but you'll have that sort of joy of learning it at the moment.

§   For [our group that's] sort of like a generative poem. It's where we started doing it, and it sort of was a grassroots discovery process. We didn't prethink it and then do it. We sort of just groped our way toward it and are still groping our way toward it.

§   I guess I've learned a lot about myself that I wasn't aware of in terms of my way of thinking. Like my obsession with details. You know, with this project we'd have brainstorming sessions and an idea would pop up and I immediately would say, "But . . ., " "Wait, let's analyze the problems," or whatever . . . rather than just sort of letting them be, you know, getting them out. And I can't say that I'm always successful in countering that, but at least I'm aware of it. . . . So that's a real benefit for me. And that's far beyond the particular thing that we're working on.

§   And a very valuable part for me was that you keyed in on where I was, so I could come in and be me. I could be a global self all over the place and that was, most of the time, OK. And then we just got, not a seesaw but a kind of balance where the two fit together.

§   Seeing that, too, makes me realize that even if she's not thinking in a way that I'm comfortable with and the way that I think you have to approach certain tasks, that there's really a lot of value in thinking in that other way.

§   [For us, the learning takes several forms.] We're learning in traditional ways by bringing books, and information and ideas from multiple sources into our conversation, but we're also learning together from a joint examination of our own personal experience. And out of that experience comes the search for new language, for new styles of writing, for new ideas that we can offer as findings, but there's somehow, for me, at least, there's a different attention to the quality of learning that is in our intention.

Steed (1994) offers an interesting insight about the learning involved in collaborative work: "We write to share our learning with others and to advance scholarly understanding of the discipline, but at the same time we write because that activity requires us to learn and to refine and articulate what we have learned. In collaborating with others, this joint learning and teaching is frequently enhanced well beyond levels that can be easily attained through solitary research and writing. There is, to borrow from economics, a type of multiplier effect in collaboration which pushes our personal understanding of the topic, and our ability to articulate that understanding, further than we might normally or reasonably do by ourselves" (p. 146).

It comes as no surprise that a group of adult educators would identify learning as such an important aspect of their experience of academic collaboration. What strikes us about the comments of these women, though, is the complexity of that learning. While our women would certainly agree with Steed, the learning they describe is more than what he points to. Theirs combines the personal and the professional, a learning that develops theoretical concepts as well as personal insights. And there's an excitement to the learning here, a degree of pure enjoyment, that seems to be foundational to the collaborative process for them.

Collaboration and Relationship

In listening to each of you describe your experiences of collaboration, we hear you talk a lot about the relationship itself. Several of you spoke about the personal friendships that became the base for your professional work together.

§   [That was definitely true for us. When we met] we started talking about our personal lives, and there was this incredible match. Even our dissertation topics were the same. We started stories [and the other would say], "Yeah, that happened [to me, too!]" From the beginning, we finished each other's sentences. [We're professionally] very complementary, both being interested in the universe of the ideas we're writing about, but each of us has some different strengths.

§   I also think, though, that we would have a relationship without the writing. The writing is just a wonderful piece of how we connect. But, I think we're people that would have found one another.

But is the relationship issue always positive?

§   Well, a real tension can develop between being concerned about the integrity and the value of the final product and the sustaining of the relationship, especially if it's a personal and professional relationship or a long-term relationship.

§   What we're saying is that all of this relationship stuff is also embedded in the collaboration. What are our principles, our ethics, and when do you take over what somebody else has started? I mean, that's part of the tension here. [Problems arise.] You're working with this person and she wants to have control of what she's written, right? Except, you also know something needs to be done, and how do you [step in]?

§   It's interesting that [in the literature on collaboration] they don't talk about this stuff at all. [They discuss the benefits, but not the struggles.] And even the struggles don't get personal; my friendship is more important than the product, and yet I want a good product, so how do I deal with both? Those are the stickier issues. So, it's not all glorious.

§   One of the things that happens when you have a long-term commitment to each other [like we do in the Group for Collaborative Inquiry] is you build up a history together of how you've made sense out of your collective, lived experience. [But] it's hard—really hard.

§   I think [that's because] a group goes through developmental stages very similar to what the individual [goes through]. I'm just thinking of Erikson's different stages. . . . Issues like trust and mistrust are messy issues, but if you're going to move beyond just doing cognitive things and try to get the whole person [involved], then these are real issues that come up. I think that's what we're really working for, to have integrity as individuals and as a group within meaning-making. But you have to go through each of the stages. You have to have a real sense of faithfulness and patience, and, I think, compassion is one of the things that's really important.

§   Well, in a sense it is countercultural, and I think that's a part of what makes it so difficult; we're a culture that builds individualism, and the academy rewards individualism, and everything feeds toward individualism and personal excellence. So everything we are doing is not just ideologically countercultural to that, but personally, in our own lives, countercultural to that. Which means that we're having to place connection in front of personal aggrandizement [all the time].

The issue of relationship is clearly central for these women; it is, as one of them said, "embedded in the collaboration," and that can be both a source of great strength and the nexus of major problems. These relational issues, as one of the group noted, don't appear much in the literature on collaboration. It is implicit, however, in some of the reflections of women academics who have collaborated.

Baker and Kline (1996), a mother-daughter collaboration on a book about feminist mothers and daughters, initially wondered, "Could we negotiate the twists and turns of our own relationship as we explored the dynamics of others'?" (p. xiii). It turned out to be a realistic concern, though not an insurmountable one. Ede and Lunsford (1988), reflecting on what it's like for close friends to write together, explore relational issues in authorship more directly. They speak of their friendship as both "powerful impetus, and subsequent reinforcement" (p. 125) for their collaboration, and they discuss how their different approaches to writing have been altered through working together. For Belenky, Clinchy, Goldberger, and Tarule, who at first knew each other only as professional associates, a major feature of how they agreed to work together involved extensive periods of contact and the development of coequal working arrangements (Ashton-Jones and Thomas, 1990).

In the literature we read and in our interviews, we saw a consistent concern with the relationship within the collaborative process. There is a sense of responsibility to the relationship that is striking here, both when it is working and when it becomes problematic. There is also a willingness to do the work necessary to make that relationship work. Clearly relationship is a central feature of the collaborative experience for women academics.

Discussion

This virtual conversation has given us significant insight into what characterizes women's experience of partnership in academic collaboration. The various elements discussed reveal a process that is diverse, highly relational, and dynamic, one that often stimulates significant learning and personal development, but also one that comes at a price. When we examined our findings within their context, namely the particular culture of academic life, we were especially struck by the cost. All of the women we interviewed and read describe intensely busy lives; all juggle multiple professional and personal responsibilities. We saw this not only in their words but also in our own interactions with them; our interviews had to be fitted into very tight schedules for all of us. Given the demands already facing these women, why would they choose to take on more work, work which takes an enormous amount of additional time and energy, is difficult in its own right, and for which they receive little credit in academic terms? Why do they willingly complicate their already complex lives?

We think that this points, once again, to the central importance of connection for women. Even in an environment that places the highest value on individual achievement, women will choose, in the words of one of our women, "to place connection in front of personal aggrandizement." As Caffarella (1992) has extensively documented, the centrality of relationships is a consistent theme in the literature on women's psychosocial development. By examining those relationships in specific contexts, we can begin to understand the meaning that they have for women.

Our findings suggest something about the meaning women give to connection in the context of academic life. It isn't enough to say that for them the benefits simply outweigh the costs. The women with whom we spoke described the collaborative process in much more personal terms. They spoke of it as if it were a living thing—a multidimensional, dynamic, energizing reality that has the potential to enrich their lives. The effort that they invest in collaboration is life-sustaining effort. While the outcome of the collaboration, the product, is not unimportant to them, they never speak of it as the sole or even the primary goal. But they do speak extensively and with some passion about the relational process and all that's involved with that in producing the final product.

We believe that this valuing of connectedness stands at the heart of the collaborative experience for these women academics. It may also be that a sense of connection is integral to the process of knowledge production for them. But it is clear that collaboration is an experience of partnering for learning that these women value highly and that will continue to play a significant role in their professional lives.

References

Aisenberg, N., and Harrington, M. *Women of Academe: Outsiders in the Sacred Grove.* Amherst: University of Massachusetts Press, 1988.

Ashton-Jones, E. "Coauthoring for Scholarly Publication: Should You Collaborate?" In J. M. Moxley (ed.), *Writing and Publishing for Academic Authors.* Lanham, Md.: University Press of America, 1992.

Ashton-Jones, E., and Thomas, D. K. "Composition, Collaboration, and Women's Ways of Knowing: A Conversation with Mary Belenky." *Journal of Advanced Composition,* 1990, *10* (2), 275–292.

Baker, C. L., and Kline, C. B. *The Conversation Begins: Mothers and Daughters Talk About Living Feminism.* New York: Bantam Books, 1996.

Baldwin, R. G., and Austin, A. R. "Toward a Greater Understanding of Faculty Research Collaboration." *Review of Higher Education,* 1995, *19* (1), 45–70.

Belenky, M. F., Clinchy, B. M., Goldberger, N. G., and Tarule, J. M. *Women's Ways of Knowing.* New York: Basic Books, 1986.

Caffarella, R. S. *Psychosocial Development of Women: Linkages to Teaching and Leadership in Adult Education.* Columbus: ERIC Clearinghouse on Adult, Career, and Vocational Education, Center on Education and Training for Employment, Ohio State University, 1992.

Ede, L. S., and Lunsford, A. A. *Singular Texts/Plural Authors: Perspectives on Collaborative Writing.* Carbondale: Southern Illinois University Press, 1990.

Gilligan, C. *In a Different Voice.* Cambridge, Mass.: Harvard University Press, 1982.

Group for Collaborative Inquiry and thINQ. "Collaborative Inquiry for the Public Arena." In A. Brooks and K. E. Watkins (eds.), *The Emerging Power of Action Inquiry Technologies.* New Directions for Adult and Continuing Education, no. 63. San Francisco: Jossey-Bass, 1994.

Hiemstra, R., and Brockett, R. G. "Collaboration, Networking, and the Research Community." In D. R. Garrison (ed.), *Research Perspectives in Adult Education.* Malabar, Fla.: Krieger, 1994.

Josselson, R. *Finding Herself: Pathways to Identity Development in Women.* San Francisco: Jossey-Bass, 1987.

Kennedy, E. L. "In Pursuit of Connection: Reflections on Collaborative Work." *American Anthropologist,* 1995, *97* (1), 26–33.

Lunsford, A. A., and Ede, L. S. "Collaboration and Compromise: The Fine Art of Writing with a Friend." In T. Waldrep (ed.), *Writers on Writing.* Vol. 2. New York: Random House, 1988.

Steed, R. P. "Collaboration in Political Science: The Research-Writing Nexus." In J. S. Leonard, C. E. Wharton, R. M. Davis, and J. Harris (eds.), *Author-ity and Textuality: Current Views of Collaborative Writing*. West Cornwall, Conn.: Locust Hill Press, 1994.

M. CAROLYN CLARK *is associate professor of adult education at Texas A&M University.*

DENISE B. WATSON *is a doctoral student in adult education at Texas A&M University.*

Overcoming habits of expectation is required of teachers and students who would engage in collaborative learning, a special type of teaching and learning in which participants engage in co-construction of new knowledge.

Collaborative Learning: People Laboring Together to Construct Knowledge

John M. Peters, Joseph L. Armstrong

"This is my way of working, of thinking. First I try to make a circle so the issue can't escape" (Horton and Freire, 1990, p. 156). Paulo Freire said that in a conversation with Myles Horton at Highlander in 1987. The two men were discussing educational practice, specifically how in their work as teachers/facilitators they were able to achieve a delicate balance between bringing out the knowledge of people while going beyond the people's knowledge. Myles spoke of a "circle of learners," in which people grow by learning with each other while co-constructing knowledge. A circle. Like Myles and Paulo and so many other adult educators, we image a circle when we think about adults learning with adults, and when we think of collaboration.

Collaboration means that people labor together in order to construct something that did not exist before the collaboration, something that does not and cannot fully exist in the lives of individual collaborators. For example, when two people collaborate in order to produce a book (as Hiemstra and Brockett in Chapter Five describe), they are in the business of creating something new—a written document that could not have existed prior to their collaborative efforts. The contents of the book cannot be reduced to what either author contributed or knew, because the book is their book, and it is more than the individual authors' contributions added together. We like to think of this result as $1 + 1 = 3$.

To say that $1 + 1 = 3$ not only means that the whole is greater than the sum of its parts, but it also means that the result is something other than the parts. When two or more people collaborate, each collaborator contributes something to the effort, and the parties jointly contribute something to the effort. There are individual contributions, and there is a group contribution. In a collaborative learning experience, individuals bring their knowledge and their actions to the table, and as members of a group, individuals contribute their collective knowledge and actions to the experience. Thus, in a collaborative learning experience, individuals learn and the group learns. The group learning experience isn't simply the sum of the individual learning experiences, however, it is both more than and other than the individual experiences.

The group learning experience is more than the sum of individual experiences because of the interactive nature of the knowledge construction process. While we have difficulty imagining how anyone can "add up" individual learners' knowledge in any case, we do believe that in the collaborative learning experience, no individual's knowledge can be expressed except in terms of what it means to the speaker *and* to someone else in the collaborative relationship. For example, when one collaborator speaks to another collaborator, the speaker intends to be understood as meaning such and such, and the listener constructs meaning based on the words uttered by the speaker, whether or not that meaning is the same as the speaker's intended meaning. This is done in the context of the *relationship* that is developed between the collaborators, a feature of collaborative learning discussed later in this chapter. The construction of knowledge within this relationship is joint knowledge construction, and is also other than the sum of individual members' knowledge.

The knowledge developed is other than the sum of individual members' knowledge because it is jointly constructed knowledge. Once the meaning of words spoken (or nonverbal gestures) is realized by people who are communicating in a collaborative relationship, what each person contributes to that construction can never be fully reconstructed. That is, once the people's talk is talked and interpretations are made, the context changes, the meaning of previously spoken words changes, and the collaborators can't "go home again." The next interpretation is made in terms of the just-developed interpretation. The meaning that is developed, as fluid as it is in a collaborative learning experience, is group meaning, something other than the individual interpretations of what the group has constructed.

In a group of collaborators, the group process moves from member to member, from member to group, and from group to member. Members don't just talk with one another. They also talk into the group and from the group. That is, as individuals talk to one another, they construct meaning from what is said and how it is said, and the result is meaning that the several people have constructed in the process of talking and interpreting, talking and interpreting, and so forth. What is jointly said and interpreted becomes the context for and the focus of further talk and interpretation.

Imagine a dozen people sitting in a circle. They are there to learn about ways of forming alliances among the adult education organizations they represent. One person in the circle, Mary, suggests that the group learn how to develop a joint marketing plan that will benefit all those who would agree to contribute to the campaign. Another person in the circle, Bob, asks Mary to say more about what she means by a marketing campaign. At this point, imagine putting an "x" between Mary and Bob. "x" is what they are talking about. Their talk is "between" them. Each is talking to the other in terms of "x." Both are talking into "x" and from "x." Now imagine that Bob has just said more about "x," and a third person, Alice, asks for additional information, and Mary obliges. The "x" now moves, relocating somewhere in the proximity of Mary, Bob, and Alice, who are interacting with one another. (You should visualize "x" as moving about the circle as different people speak. Drawing lines between the speakers helps, so that "x" can more easily be located on the lines, on intersecting points, in areas defined by triads, and so forth.) When all or nearly all other members of the group (say, Tom, Bill, Sarah, and James) speak into and from "x," it can be seen as located near the center of the circle. If "x" is what the circle of people are talking about, "x" can be understood as what the group knows, or simply as the momentary product of what they have worked to construct by verbally and nonverbally interacting with one another.

By identifying and locating "x" between speakers and ultimately in the center of a group, the emphasis on what is going on shifts from a focus on individuals to a focus on the relationship among members of the group. No individual has a monopoly on what is going on, although as each individual expresses himself or herself, what the group "sees" also changes. The issue, topic, problem, plan, or whatever the group's focus might be, is not in the head of anyone in the group, is not owned by anyone in the group, but is instead understood in terms of the relationship among members of the group and as the group's own creation. On achieving this focus, the group can build on its own meaning of what it has constructed, as long as the group exists.

Relationship and Content

We have made several references to the relationship among participants in a collaborative learning experience, and we have indicated that in every teaching-learning experience there is also content, or a topic, or simply information, involved (for instance, the marketing plan, or "x" in the above example). The interaction of participants that leads to knowledge construction can be understood in terms of the interaction between relationship and content. According to Watzlawick, Beavin, and Jackson (1967), "Every communication has a content and a relationship aspect, such that the latter classifies the former and is therefore a metacommunication" (p. 54). What the authors mean by this is that content does not have meaning except in terms of the intentions of the people who are communicating with one another and the nature of the relationship that they construct in the process of communicating. They go on to say that "Any communication implies a commitment and thereby defines the relationship. . . . A communication not only conveys information, but at the same time it imposes behavior" (p. 51). The latter aspect of communication refers to "what sort of message it is to be taken as, and, therefore, ultimately to the relationship between the communicants. All such relationship statements are about one or several of the following assertions: 'This is how I see myself . . . this is how I see you . . . this is how I see you seeing me . . .' and so forth in theoretically infinite regress" (p. 51).

To say that the content (information) of an utterance is a function of the nature of the relationship established among collaborators is to suggest that the meaning of what is said in an interaction varies with how the relationship itself is understood. For example, the unequal distribution of power and authority in a group can profoundly influence the direction of decision making and knowledge construction. The involvement of a teacher in a collaborative learning group can implicate several different outcomes, depending on how the teacher is seen by students[1] in terms of her authority as teacher, as subject matter expert, as leader of the group. Unless the teacher sees herself as a co-constructor of knowledge and acts on that perception, she is likely to be seen by students as the primary source of knowledge and thus their own role in knowledge construction would be limited to interpreting whatever the teacher says. If an upper-level business executive is present whenever a group of mid-management level personnel collaborate on sensitive corporate issues, the nature of their collaboration is likely to be other than it would be if the executive were absent (Argyris, 1994).

Three Types of Teaching and Learning

Teaching-learning settings in adult education vary greatly, but they can be understood in part by the types of relationships between teachers and learners involved in those settings. In the interest of locating collaborative learning in the various forms of teaching and learning, we describe these in terms of three types, described in detail in our book *Facilitating Collaborative Learning* (Peters and Armstrong, in press). A synopsis of these types of teaching and learning follows, and that discussion is followed by a list of strategies that we find effective as we facilitate collaborative learning experiences in our own work settings.

We describe three types of teaching and learning. We call Type One "teaching by transmission, learning by reception." In Type One, the relationships are principally between the teacher and students, such that the direction of communication is from the teacher to the students. The teacher has information that he or she assumes students need. Usually, the students do not participate in the selection of content, nor do they control the nature of the relationship between themselves and the teacher. They accept the relationship set by the teacher, or they choose not to participate in it. Assessment of what the students receive from the experience is usually accomplished in terms of what the teacher expects, within the context of a predetermined set of topics, a discipline, or the subject matter, usually institutionally bound. The principal mode associated with this type is the lecture. The focus of Type One teaching and learning is individual learning.

Type Two teaching and learning is "teaching by transmission, learning by sharing." In Type Two, the role of the teacher is to transmit information and to enable students to transmit information to one another and sometimes to the teacher. The relationships established are between the teacher and students and among students. The teacher is the primary source of information, but not the sole source. The student is sometimes both a learner and a teacher, transmitting information as well as receiving it. The mode of teaching and learning commonly associated with Type Two is lecture followed by discussion, although the mode can vary. The range of content domains accommodated by Type Two is usually greater than by Type One, as there is more opportunity for students to share personal experiences and interpretations of subject matter brought to the setting by the teacher. The focus of Type Two is individual learning.

Type Three teaching and learning is distinguished not only by a focus on joint construction of knowledge, but also by the designation of the teacher as a member of the group of learners and by the role of the group in the learning experience. The teacher is one of the participants in a collaborative learning experience. The teacher may and usually does have special knowledge of content, but his or her knowledge does not necessarily supersede that of the other learners in the group. The teacher usually will have special knowledge of and skills as a facilitator of collaborative learning. One or more of the other learners may also have similar facilitator knowledge and skills or will learn how to serve as facilitator at some point in the group's learning experience. In Type Three, the relationship is defined in terms of learner to learner, learner to group, and group to learner. Dialogue is the principal mode of discourse associated with Type Three, although modes associated with Types One (for example, a presentation by a teacher) and Two (for example, a discussion) can also be present in a Type Three teaching-learning experience. A teacher presentation or student sharing of information during a discussion means that information is both transmitted and received by participants in the process, but the primary aim of their interaction is the construction of new knowledge. The focus of Type Three is both individual and group learning.

The three types of teaching and learning implicate different roles for teachers and learners. They also suggest different views of knowledge and knowing. Clearly, Type One is the dominant type, and its dominance has a lot to do with choices that teachers and learners make between this type and the other two.

Implications for Teachers and Students

The dominance of Type One teaching and learning in educational organizations and in noneducational organizations in which education is a secondary activity is grounded in a worldview that supports the teacher as authority, knowledge as a commodity, and the learner as an empty or nearly empty vessel. Adults, whether teachers or learners, are quite familiar with how this dominant model works. We have been schooled in it for most of our lives. Type One is schooling. It is also training, in most places, and it is most of higher education.

Type Two teaching and learning represents hope—hope that the cooperative learning movement that is once again rearing its progressive head will prevail in more and more schools; hope that the adult educators who have proudly "discovered" experience-based learning will somehow convince enough others that the most important factor in the learning process is what the learner already knows or is able to do; hope that more professors will recognize that all learners, especially adult learners, bring to classrooms a great deal that can be exploited by teachers and other learners who would learn from and with one another. However, although these are steps in the right direction, present models of cooperative education and experiential learning do not go far enough in terms of their emphasis on the joint construction of new knowledge that leads to both group and individual learning.

Type Three teaching and learning does aim for joint construction of new knowledge by groups and individuals, but very little of this type occurs in most institutions of teaching and learning. One reason for this relative lack of Type Three activity is the sheer power of the Type One way of thinking on the part of teachers and students alike. Type Three, collaborative learning, requires people who would learn collaboratively to get over some of the hang-ups and myths associated with Type One and Type Two teaching and learning. Once past their own assumptions about how teachers are supposed to act, how learners are supposed to learn, and how knowledge is made, teachers and learners alike can begin to taste the fruits of collaborative learning.

Type Three teaching and learning is a way of learning that doesn't work by the same rules as the other two types, precisely because it is a different way of learning, with different concepts: people laboring together to construct new knowledge, group knowledge and individual knowledge. In this setting, a teacher can't be the sole source of knowledge. There is no way that one person can know it all, much less know what is about to be constructed as new knowledge. No one in the group can know that. But everyone in the group knows something, usually a lot, which is a possible aspect of the would-be, soon-to-be-constructed knowledge.

Nearly all of us enter into a teaching-learning situation with Type One backgrounds and Type One expectations. The image of teacher as transmitter of information and the image of student as receiver of information accompanies us to all three types of teaching and learning. When the images and the type of teaching and learning clash, however, the result can be disappointing for both teachers and students. The disappointment is based on misplaced expectations.

Students expecting Type One teaching in a Type Two environment may be frustrated when they perceive information exchanged among students to be less valuable than what the teacher could offer as subject matter expert. Thus, students may consider time given to student interaction to be wasted time, and the opportunity for meaningful knowledge construction is lost on the very people who have the most to gain from it. The possibility of this barrier to teaching and learning is made even greater by the perceived role of the teacher as authority in both Type One and Type Two teaching and learning. In both types, what is to be learned and how it is to be learned are usually chosen by the teacher. So are the rewards and punishments (for example, grades, approval, and other reinforcers) that are meted out to students. Moreover, the teacher is often an agent of an organization that itself might also be important in the lives of students (for instance, degree-granting organizations or employers offering training programs). Given the primacy of the teacher's subject matter authority and the possibility that the organization sponsoring the event has control over what the student wants, the relationship between teacher and students is defined in terms of a difference in power. The institutionalization of this imbalance in power is the basis of the dominance of Type One teaching and learning.

One of the outcomes of institutionalization of Type One teaching and learning is the teacher's concern with "covering content." There may be a curriculum involved, perhaps state regulations or certification requirements. The sponsoring institution may be concerned with transfer credits between institutions of higher education, or there may a perceived need to fit each course in a program into the structure of requirements, and so on. Under these circumstances, who can blame a teacher for being paranoid about not covering content, only to be caught not preparing students adequately for the system's own requirements?

Teachers are usually expected to choose the content, to determine its scope, sequence, and how it is to be integrated (see Tyler, 1950). We respect the choices made by teachers who practice by these expectations, as we believe that there is ample room for all three types of teaching and learning in the world of education. However, there are situations in which the best choice that teachers can make is to engage with students in a collaborative learning experience. Given a choice, for the Type One teacher this nearly always starts with the teacher needing to have the courage to "let go of the reins." One of our colleagues demonstrated this courage just the other day. . . .

A college professor told us that he is teaching a psychology course in which K–12 teacher interns (soon to be K–12 teachers) are enrolled. A particular textbook is required for the course, the same one required in other sections of the course taught by other professors, but the professor of our acquaintance said that he merely asks the course participants to read the text and other materials, and he asks them, in class, what stands out for them in their readings. This is to get the conversation among them going. Teacher and learners alike jump into a discussion and sometimes dialogue about a topic or two drawn from what stood out for a couple of people. When we asked the professor, "How do you ensure that the content is covered?" he replied that he doesn't particularly worry about that, since he would rather sacrifice breadth for depth in knowledge as it relates to textbook topics. In other words, he admitted that he and the other participants in the course couldn't possibly talk about all of the topics in the book but could do most of them during the semester, and for those that were discussed, they would be discussed in greater depth. Besides, he said, how much detail do learners retain a few weeks past the semester's end?

This is a case of a teacher making a choice—a choice of ways to look at the role of teacher, a teacher's responsibility to teach, a choice of types of teaching and learning. One could argue that this teacher is secure enough to try almost anything, but others may have good reason to hold on to their traditional role as type one teacher and run few, if any, risks. So the hurdle facing many Type One teachers may be one of risk taking and willingness to experiment with alternative ways of teaching.

Students entering a Type Three teaching-learning experience are likely to find a teacher who operates by a different set of expectations, but the students themselves may be frustrated by the opportunity laid before them. They may initially suspect that the teacher lacks competence in his or her subject matter. Like teachers accustomed to Type One processes, students' Type One expectations can easily delay or even prevent their collaborative learning experience. In our own courses, the first few class sessions are often cluttered with false starts and fragments of failed intentions, as we and students sort out what collaborative learning means to all of us. (As facilitators, we are not always secure in our response to questions that amount to, "What do you want us to learn and will you tell us when and how well we learned what you will teach us?" Or the classic, "Is there a test?" We bring Type One baggage to the classroom, too.) In one of our classes, a student new to collaborative learning said, "I know how to go to school. But now you are changing the rules on me." Among other things, she was saying that she knew how to manage school in concert with her job, her family, and her other adult responsibilities. However, her management strategy depended on school being a matter of going to class, taking notes, identifying the teacher's expectations, fulfilling them, and moving on to the next course. Suddenly, she found herself in a teaching-learning environment in which few of her expectations applied.

In working with students in such a setting, we have experimented with several approaches that are beginning to work for us and students with whom we collaborate. Following are some of the ways we approach our work in graduate and undergraduate courses:

- We try to get students involved in an episode of collaborative learning as early in the course as possible. This usually means that all of us get involved in constructing new knowledge from a story, a critical incident, a learning autobiography, a news event, a book author's claim, or whatever suits the nature of the course we are dealing with. Our intent is to structure the initial experience so that students can get into collaborative learning and then learn how they are learning what they are learning. We want them to be able to take action as collaborators, and to reflect on that action. We really haven't found a better way to get going than to get going. Telling any group of people how to learn collaboratively and expecting them to apply what they are told seems to us to be a contradiction in intent, or perhaps in types. Besides,

that approach hasn't worked for us. We and the students need to jointly construct what for most of the group is a new way of learning.

- We take every opportunity to "point out" when we or others in the group
are doing something to promote a collaborative learning experience. Ultimately, we want members of the group to "catch themselves" collaborating.
We take time to jointly and openly reflect on what we are doing and how
we are doing it.

- We try to show the utmost respect for everyone in the group and everything
that is said by anyone in the group. By demonstrating this early in the
course, there is a greater than average chance that all members of the group
will follow suit and show respect for one another.

- We're not really sure whether trust follows respect or vice versa, but trust
has to be in the mix along with respect. People in collaborative relationships
take a risk when opening their thoughts and feelings to one another, and
trust is built when the risk taker receives positive regard from the others for
ideas expressed, inquiries made, and feelings shared. Initially, we as teach-
ers/facilitators must do everything we can to demonstrate trust, which
includes trusting ourselves in the process. Eventually, as trust develops and
spreads through the group, we can more easily enter the group as a trusted
co-constructor of knowledge.

- As facilitators, we have found that we need to know even more content than
we do as lecturers. In lecturing, (as in Type One and Type Two situations),
we can restrict what we have to say to a prepared plan and pretty much control what is said and discussed in a class experience. By being "in charge" we
can direct what happens. However, in a collaborative learning experience in
which the knowledge that is constructed is never predictable, we can never
really be fully prepared to share our subject matter expertise about whatever
comes up. Neither can we deny our expertise or shun our responsibility as
teachers. Thus, we discovered early on that we have to be overprepared at
all times, in terms of content and process, so that whatever we have to offer
the group in the way of information can be shared when appropriate to the
knowledge construction process.

- The relationship among collaborators is vital to the process of collaborative
learning. We work to keep group members' focus on what goes on "in
between" collaborators, as discussed earlier in this chapter. (We like to keep
the issue in the center of the circle.) We have found that, by focusing on the
"x," we can move more quickly to the group learning stage than if we reinforce the Type One belief that everything important in learning occurs in the
heads of individuals. Initially, when we as facilitators "see" group learning
occur, we "stop the music" and help students reflect on what we have just
done, to reinforce that aspect of the collaborative learning experience.

- As a course progresses, we try to facilitate what we call a "level-izing" process;
that is, we want all of us to see ourselves learning, and to see ourselves seeing ourselves learning (we "look down" from above on what we are doing
in a group). As we described earlier, learning for us involves content and

relationship. Content is a function of relationship and all that it involves. Collaborators need to attend to how they are learning what they are learning. Thus, we frequently "stop the music" so that all of us can take a look at the nature of the relationships we form in our experience, and how the variations in those relationships help constitute what is being learned. By this means, we learn how we are learning, and that in turn helps shape our relationships, and the relationships shape what we are learning, and so forth. This is accomplished by pointing out and by reflecting openly about our experiences as we are having them.

Conclusion

The three types of teaching and learning we describe in this chapter may or may not capture the full range of adult education enterprises, but we wanted to set the context for our particular concern for the dynamics of collaborative learning. We believe that the emphasis on joint construction of knowledge, on the teacher/facilitator as a collaborator, and on group learning distinguishes collaborative learning, or Type Three, from the other types of teaching and learning. Type Three teaching and learning is not commonly found in practice among teachers and learners in formal education institutions, or even in adult education. What passes for collaborative learning is usually Type Two teaching and learning.

We claim that adult educators and students who seek to engage in collaborative learning are often frustrated because of the long-term effects of our schooling in Type One and Type Two teaching and learning. We therefore face a few bumps in the road along the way. Foremost among these bumps are habits of expectation—such as the ones that concern the proper role of the teacher as transmitter of knowledge and the role of the student as receiver of knowledge—and the power relationships that traditional role expectations often create. For example, with power comes responsibility, and when the teacher relinquishes some of his or her power and the power of the student increases, the student also must also assume greater responsibility for what happens in a teaching-learning experience.

There are also epistemological hurdles to deal with, as teachers and students redefine their teaching-learning relationships, particularly as they concern how knowledge is made. A circle of learners is likely to include diverse views on the nature of knowledge and how it comes to be knowledge, as well as on what is expected of those in the circle. As teachers/facilitators concerned with what goes on in this circle, we urge other adult educators to take a seat next to us.

Note

1. Since teachers are also learners, we use the term "student" throughout this chapter to refer to people who are not teachers but who participate with a teacher in formal learning experiences.

References

Argyris, C. "Good Communication That Blocks Learning." *Harvard Business Review,* July–Aug. 1994, pp. 77–85.

Horton, M., and Freire, P. *We Make the Road by Walking: Conversations on Education and Social Change.* Philadelphia: Temple University Press, 1990.

Peters, J. M., and Armstrong, J. L. *Facilitating Collaborative Learning.* San Francisco: Jossey-Bass, in press.

Tyler, R. W. *Basic Principles of Curriculum and Instruction.* Chicago: University of Chicago Press, 1950.

Watzlawick, P., Beavin, J. H., and Jackson, D. D. *Pragmatics of Human Communication.* New York: Norton, 1967.

JOHN M. PETERS is professor and coordinator of the doctoral program in collaborative learning at the University of Tennessee, Knoxville.

JOSEPH L. ARMSTRONG is assistant professor of adult education at Morehead State University in Morehead, Kentucky.

The power of a collaborative partnership is derived from the synergy created when human beings connect in productive, meaningful activity.

Human Connections

Angela Sgroi, Iris M. Saltiel

We started this project with a relatively mundane curiosity about how different kinds of collaborations and partnerships can support learning. But we continue to be surprised at the unusually high level of interest in the subject. There is an attraction to this idea of learning together through collaboration, through partnerships, mentorships, and teams, that is more than a fad. There is a basic need for people-to-people connections in the educational process to fulfill some unidentified longing.

Our intention in this volume was to look for collaborations and partnerships in different contexts, or to look from a different perspective at some of those in more common contexts. It was also our intent to try to focus the discussions on the interactions between and among partners, especially based on the questions laid out in the Editors' Notes. The chapters in this sourcebook take us inside collaborations and partnerships formed in traditional arts classes and university classrooms, in graduate program mentorships that became peer partnerships, as well as inside peer partnerships in formal degree programs, in professional research, and in the writing of literature.

Key Elements

The types of interactions are significantly different in the case of each chapter of this volume, but we have identified certain commonalities. These are key elements of collaborative partnerships: (1) Implicit in every successful collaborative partnership is a deep trust and respect for each member. (2) Thus, successful collaborative partners must select each other. (3) The driving force behind successful collaborative partnerships is the power of ideas and dreams—the mutual striving toward common goals. Linked to this is the shared belief that members can be more productive and effective together than

New Directions for Adult and Continuing Education, no. 79, Fall 1998 © Jossey-Bass Publishers

alone. (4) This is based, in part, on the fact that the partners are equal but different, having complementary personality traits and qualities. (5) It is also based on the fact that there is a synergy between them. The next section of this chapter develops these key elements as they are reflected in the chapters of this book.

Deep Trust and Respect. The qualities of trust and respect are not always articulated in partner relationships. However, if they are not there, the partnership does not exist. It is, no doubt, a part of how and why partners select each other. It is certainly one factor that keeps them working toward their common goal. It is the basic element in the belief that they can accomplish more together than they can alone.

The artists and students from collaborative initiatives trust that their teacher/partners are masters of the knowledge base of their fields and know not only what knowledge and skills the neophytes need to learn, but also how to help them achieve that learning. They also trust their teacher/partners to care enough about them as learners to give honest feedback and evaluation and to generally lead them on the right path. The peer partners have selected a partner whom they trust to have certain knowledge, skills, and good judgment.

There is a strong connection between collaborative partnerships and personal relationships, which is linked to the trust and respect that collaborative partners feel toward one another. For some collaborative partners, the trust and respect are limited to the expertise and abilities in each other needed to accomplish the work goals. For most, however, the trust and respect in the collaborative partnership either develop from or extend into a full personal and professional relationship.

For example, when Katzenbach and Smith (1993) describe the characteristics of teams, they stress the centrality of significant performance challenges. "Performance . . . is the primary objective, while a team remains the means, not the end. Performance is the crux of the matter for teams" (p. 12). Trust on teams, on the other hand, develops as a result of working toward a common goal. It is not necessarily present at the outset of the relationship. "Real teams do not develop until the people in them work hard to overcome barriers that stand in the way of collective performance. By surmounting such obstacles together, people on teams build trust and confidence in each other's capabilities" (p. 18). The class situations described by Peters and Armstrong are most likely to follow this model.

Although having a common goal is necessary to most of the other partnerships described in this volume, it is not always the primary purpose of the relationship. Some partnerships end when the task is completed, but many extend beyond the individual project to other projects, and directly into the personal lives of the partners. Saltiel, Hiemstra and Brockett, Clark and Watson, and Owenby all describe partnerships in which the working relationship is critical, yet the partnership is more than a working relationship. For many of the partnerships described in this book, the relationship aspect is as important or even more important than the work aspect.

Successful Partners Select Each Other. Partners select each other to work with. Often it is instinctive; they sense that they will be able to work together. Hiemstra and Brockett (Chapter Five) describe it best: "Sometimes it is the result of a common vision. At other times, it comes from a mutual desire to interact with another like-minded person." Most times the relationship builds slowly, trust and a common goal laying the foundation for working together.

Certainly evidenced when Hiemstra and Brockett discuss their evolving partnership and friendship is the idea that they chose each other to work with. Clark and Watson explore how female academics choose one another to work with in their research. Saltiel discovered how partnerships are formed unintentionally in her work with adult students. The human element of "I knew the first time I saw her that we would get along" helps to illustrate the quirky nature of these partnerships.

Conversely, Sgroi found that teachers and learners in the arts were clear that not all teacher-learner relationships are partnerships. When they form, it is because they select each other. Even when the collaboration is formed by the professor, the learning is more powerful when compatible relationships are formed. In both of these contexts, a more powerful and intense learning experience results from people "connecting" intellectually.

Shared Goal or Purpose. A shared vision gives the partners something to aspire to. The common goal provides the glue that cements the relationship together, and as the process of working together unfolds, the strength of the shared goal often determines the success of the partnership. This is especially critical in the goal-oriented demands of research collaborations described by Witte and James. Owenby gives us a behind-the-scenes look at the marriage of Virginia and Robert Heinlein, showing us how Virginia devoted her life to the research and other unseen work behind the publication of all of Robert's books.

Of course, for Saltiel's peer partners the shared goal was completion of their formal education program. The goals for the student artists who form learning partnerships with their teachers are the development of craft and artistic sensibility, and often overall personal development for both partners. For Peters and Armstrong's university classes, it is the joint creation of knowledge. For Hiemstra and Brockett, as well as for the women researchers interviewed by Clark and Watson, the immediate goals were important, but seem secondary to the relationship itself.

Complementary but Different. Collaborative partners usually complement each other in temperament and style as well as in skills and knowledge. Saltiel describes the unique camaraderie between individuals. One pushes toward the goal; the other may pull off in a different direction. The relationship stretches like a rubber band and either returns to its original goal or sets a better one.

Clark and Watson's chapter eloquently describes how the research partners bring their differences to the work, then weave these differences into a unique work. The Heinleins' relationship is a perfect example of a balance of two partners contributing totally different skills and knowledge to achieve successful results. Even the teacher-learner relationships in the arts provide us with examples of complementary knowledge, skills, and needs working together to make the relationship worthwhile to all partners.

Synergy Between Partners.   Sparks fly, and the energy between partners is sufficient to light up a room—or at least a book or other project. Hiemstra and Brockett provide a good inside look at this in their description of writing side by side, with one dictating and one keying the material into the computer, one idea and sentence building on the other. The women researchers in Clark and Watson's chapter describe a very similar process.

Implications for Practice

Beyond exploring and offering some insights into the inner workings of partnerships, we expected to be able to offer some recommendations for incorporating these insights into practice. The personal, intimate approach to partnerships taken in this sourcebook yielded fascinating information, but an obvious problem immediately emerged. How does one set up a learning situation in which partners can really select each other? What can a teacher do to help partners trust and respect each other? Where does synergy come from, and how can it be injected into a relationship? Of course, we do not have the answers to these perhaps unanswerable questions.

We have given this considerable thought, however, and we think that we have identified a direction that might lead to solutions. The seed of this direction comes from something Katzenbach and Smith discuss: "If there is new insight to be derived from the solid base of common sense about teams, it is the strange paradox of application. Many people simply do not apply what they already know about teams in any disciplined way, and thereby miss the performance potential before them" (p. 3).

Perhaps the best approach is to fold the difficulties into the approach. Do not expect learning partnerships to form or to be successful for every learning project. Allow flexibility. Arrange the learning situation so that learners can identify their goals and be supported in collaborative working situations if they choose them, but do not require it. Set up the learning environment so that partnerships, collaborations, or individual efforts are equally supported.

For those determined to ask students to work together in pairs, based on what we have observed in our work with partners, we refer back to Katzenbach and Smith's observations of teams that must operate in similar situations. We conclude that the partnership has a better chance of developing if the assignment has clearly focused goals that are meaningful to the partners.

Closing Reflections

At the beginning of this chapter we say that the power of collaborative partnerships lies in members' belief that together they can achieve what cannot be accomplished alone. This is so important to everything we have learned about collaborations and partnerships that we would like to discuss it further here. Clark and Watson (Chapter Seven) talk about "the central importance of connection for women": "They spoke of [the collaborative process] as if it were a living thing—a multidimensional, dynamic, energizing reality that has the potential to enrich their lives. The effort that they invest in collaboration is life-sustaining effort. While the outcome of the collaboration, the product, is not unimportant to them, they never speak of it as the sole or even the primary goal. But they do speak extensively and with some passion about the relational process and all that's involved with that in producing the final product.

Clark and Watson capture the essence of collaboration so eloquently that we repeat it here to illustrate our point. These women not only get the job of research done, they also engage in the collaborative process for its own sake. Their involvement in the collaborative process is more than a pleasant association; it is a "life-sustaining effort."

This is a remarkable conclusion. Yet, based on what we have observed in the relationships in each of the chapters, we can see this level of meaning and satisfaction in many if not all of the collaborative partnerships described. By asking authors to focus on that aspect of the collaboration or partnership they present, we were afforded the opportunity to glimpse deeper meaning and motivations.

What we saw inspired us to probe and learn about the magic of collaborative partnerships. The synergy in the relationships yielded an intense energy and deep satisfaction that seems to meet a need that is not easily identifiable.

Gregory Cajete (1994) includes the notion of connection in his devastating indictment of mainstream education in the United States and perhaps offers insight into the need driving some of the connections that humans make with each other: "The orchestrated 'bottom-line, real world' chorus sung by many in business and government has become the common refrain of those who announce *they lead* the world. Yet, what underlies the crisis of American education is the crisis of modern man's identity and his cosmological disconnection from the natural world. Those who identify most with the bottom line often suffer from an image without substance, technique without soul, and knowledge without context. The cumulative psychological result is usually alienation, loss of community, and a deep sense of incompleteness" (p. 26).

Perhaps a problem for mainstream U.S. culture (and therefore, for the educational system that attempts to communicate that culture) is that it has *no* metaphor, *no* story, *no* soul. It is simply the empty shell that is left when all of the cultures and the values that make up this country are ignored or denied, and when concern for products and structures replaces investment in and concern for people.

The potential and power of collaborative partnerships is the power of humanity. It is the power of human touch, the life force emitted and exchanged between human beings through physical, intellectual, and emotional pathways. We give energy and life to one another. This is at the heart of understanding the power of collaborative partnerships. In the end, the idea of human connections seems to be the common denominator of the examples in this sourcebook as well as in the varied works reviewed in the first chapter. These human connections give us our humanity, which, as a society, we are in desperate need of. If, as Ralph Waldo Emerson suggests, "Life is a search after power," then one of the places we find such power is in our successful collaborative partnerships.

References

Cajete, G. A. *Look to the Mountain: An Ecology of Indigenous Education.* Durango, Colo.: Kivaki Press, 1994.

Katzenbach, J. R., and Smith, D. K. *The Wisdom of Teams: Creating the High-Performance Organization.* Boston: Harvard Business School Press, 1993.

ANGELA SGROI is executive assistant to the vice president for academic affairs at The College of New Jersey, working primarily to support faculty research and teaching.

IRIS M. SALTIEL works in a corporate university at Synovus Service Corp., Columbus, Georgia.

INDEX

ORDERING INFORMATION

NEW DIRECTIONS FOR ADULT AND CONTINUING EDUCATION is a series of paperback books that explores issues of common interest to instructors, administrators, counselors, and policy makers in a broad range of adult and continuing education settings—such as colleges and universities, extension programs, businesses, the military, prisons, libraries, and museums. Books in the series are published quarterly in Spring, Summer, Fall, and Winter and are available for purchase by subscription and individually.

SUBSCRIPTIONS cost $56.00 for individuals (a savings of 35 percent over single-copy prices) and $99.00 for institutions, agencies, and libraries. Standing orders are accepted. New York residents, add local sales tax for subscriptions. (For subscriptions outside the United States, add $7.00 for shipping via surface mail or $25.00 for air mail. Orders must be prepaid in U.S. dollars by check drawn on a U.S. bank or charged to VISA, MasterCard, or American Express.)

SINGLE COPIES cost $23.00 plus shipping (see below) when payment accompanies order. California, New Jersey, New York, and Washington, D.C., residents, please include appropriate sales tax. Canadian residents, add GST and any local taxes. Billed orders will be charged shipping and handling. No billed shipments to post office boxes. (Orders from outside the United States must be prepaid in U.S. dollars by check drawn on a U.S. bank or charged to VISA, MasterCard, or American Express.)

SHIPPING (SINGLE COPIES ONLY): $30.00 and under, add $5.50; to $50.00, add $6.50; to $75.00, add $7.50; to $100.00, add $9.00; to $150.00, add $10.00.

ALL PRICES are subject to change.

DISCOUNTS FOR QUANTITY ORDERS are available. Please write to the address below for information.

ALL ORDERS must include either the name of an individual or an official purchase order number. Please submit your order as follows:
   Subscriptions: specify series and year subscription is to begin
   Single copies: include individual title code (such as ACE 59)

MAIL ALL ORDERS TO:
Jossey-Bass Publishers
350 Sansome Street
San Francisco, CA 94104–1342

Phone subscriptions or single-copy orders toll-free at (888) 378–2537 or at (415) 433–1767 (toll call).
Fax orders toll-free to: (800) 605–2665.

FOR SUBSCRIPTION SALES OUTSIDE OF THE UNITED STATES, contact any international subscription agency or Jossey-Bass directly.